Desperate Measures

Best Regards,

Michael Antravia

▲
Mike in Hong Kong.

Desperate Measures

Michael Intravia

WORD PUBLISHING
Dallas·London·Vancouver·Melbourne

DESPERATE MEASURES

Printed in the United States of America

Library of Congress Cataloging in Publication Data

Intravia, Michael, 1953–
    Desperate measures / Michael Intravia.
       p.   cm.
    ISBN 0-8499-0732-2
    1. Private investigators—Missouri. 2. Children of God (Movement)
  3. Shillander family. 4. Intravia, Michael, 1953– . I. Title.
    HV8096.M8I58 1990
    362.82'97'092—dc20
    [B]   90-46933
                                    CIP

0 1 2 3 9 AGF 1 9 8 7 6 5 4 3 2 1

To the special people in my life whose support and deep affection have been directly responsible for any success I've had. Through this dedication I hope to express my gratitude, love, and respect for them:

My wife, Patti, and my children, Tanya and Erica, for all their love, patience, and understanding.

My parents, Serfino and Louise Intravia, for the countless lessons and gifts they have provided me in life.

Robert Burke, a mentor and a friend, for providing a world of wisdom, experience, and friendship.

Acknowledgments

There are many people who have been directly or indirectly responsible for this book.

First, I want to give special thanks to Scott Biondo, whose courage and dedication made a happy ending possible.

Thanks also to the employees and clients of Allied Intelligence; to Larry Brown; Allen Carter; Terry Coleman; Brad Beckstrom; Senator Larry Pressler; Steve Haugard; all those who helped in Thailand; Alice Pifer; Ken Black; and Rex Burlison.

Others deserving of recognition include Judy Hoffman; William, Joe, Terri, and John Hoffman; Marty Reisman; John Dillmann; John and Anita Reeves; Bess and Leonard McBrayer; Lea, Ethan, and Micah Lewis; Lake Headley; Joe and Linda Lewandowski; the Blackledges; Charles and Rudy Ced; Betty Duke; and Jim Gosdin.

I'm indebted to many people: Paul Bielicki; Mary Givens; Carol and Renè Menard; Jim Carmichael; Theodore Schechter; Jeff Schechter; Ellen Watkins; Tom Devoto; Bob Devoto; Mary Ann and Marvin Barr; John and Becky Intravia; Joe and Francine Intravia; William and Jane Bazzle; Kevin and Colleen Craig; Bob and Sandy Bazzle; Ed Beagan; Blanche Wells; Cass Bank; the Berkeley Police Department; Don Kissell; Bob Cope; John Jennings; Pat Jennings; Dave Battle; Wayne Shoenberg; Ralph Kalish, Jr.; Eicardo Venturini; Bruno Rolland; Hilda Matthews; Ida Geraghty; and Teri Schuchman.

Contents

Prologue

THE TWO THAI SOLDIERS arrived with a clatter and screech of brakes via armored van. We—my friend Scott Biondo and I—spotted them immediately through the big wrought-iron gate, the worst of our fears come true. We had known the soldiers might hunt us down, had hoped with every ounce of our beings that they wouldn't.

For just an instant in the light of their opened doors we caught a glimpse of them. They wore camouflage fatigues and carried grenades in their belts and .45 caliber automatics in their hands. Then the doors slammed shut and we couldn't see any more.

More frightening, there was nothing to hear. It was 2 A.M. this February 1, 1988, a black, moonless Asian early morning, suddenly everything eerily quiet, like the deepest recesses of a catacomb; the wind and the creatures had stopped stirring. I had experienced such a stillness once before in my life, as a boy: right before a tornado struck.

This absolute absence of sound scored as more remarkable and infinitely more dangerous because men caused it. The soldiers silenced even the crickets.

Scott and I had been standing a nervous watch inside the compound of the Baptist Guest House on the outskirts of Bangkok, an enclosure completely encircled by a high wall, but now we scurried to the corner of the hostelry's wing closest to the front. I knew the soldiers would enter the property through the gate. Scaling the wall was possible but hazardous because of broken glass permanently concreted on the top.

I had no doubt the soldiers were coming in, that we were their prey, and that they intended to kill us. Maybe not here in the yard—did they care that it wouldn't look good, gunning us down in this place run by American missionaries?—but out in some remote jungle after a terror-filled ride. My hands were clammy, my mouth turned dry as dust, and visions of death squads filled my mind.

I didn't doubt, either, that Colonel Thu Lee had sent these soldiers. This brutal renegade military officer commanded forces on the Laos and Cambodian borders, where war still raged, but the dread he inspired extended even to the capital city. The mere mention of his name prompted sidelong glances and lowered voices. Corrupt and violent, Thu Lee operated more like an ancient warlord than a modern professional military man.

And he was a friend of our greatest enemy.

We edged along the wall toward the gate, taking advantage of the heavy vegetation and trees that offered only partial concealment.

Dressed in dark clothing, crouched behind a short date palm, we stared through the fanlike branches. Suddenly a light moved in the courtyard, and then two lights stretched briefly across the lawn. I peered into the dark, *willing* myself to see.

Each soldier toted a flashlight in one hand, a .45 in the other. They crept side by side across the yard, parallel to the vegetation where Scott and I hid. He glanced at me as they drew close, and I shook my head. Ambushing soldiers did not seem a good idea.

But what was? Thai authorities would take an extremely dim view of any self-defense moves we took against military personnel, no matter how malign their intentions. Besides, we weren't armed; so aggressive actions would have to catch them swiftly and unaware, at best a fifty-fifty proposition. As their army boots crunched blades of grass within a few yards of us, we focused on them in the dark like radar fixed on a target.

They stopped and began talking in Thai. Trying to stay still as a cat, I strained to control my breathing and make out the words.

One of the soldiers, his face round and pockmarked, turned and looked in our direction, and I believed we were dead meat. Instead of rapidly calculating avenues of escape— there really weren't any—my mind took a turn on its own, flashing back to the strange circumstances that had brought me ten thousand miles from a comfortable St. Louis, Missouri, suburb to this godforsaken patch of ground in Southeast Asia.

▲
Mike and Vallop.

Desperate Measures

Streets of Bangkok.

1

Here We Go Again

I CAN CLOSE MY EYES and remember every detail of that June 22, 1987 morning in St. Louis when the case of the missing children began. The day had dawned bright and beautiful and gotten better, no hint of the dark, perilous investigation awaiting us.

Everyone in the office seemed to be in a good mood, and business had never been better at Allied Intelligence, Inc., the private investigation and protective services agency I head. I was reviewing cases and approving reports to be mailed to clients when the telephone intercom rang.

"Mike," said my secretary, Joyce Henderson, "Jackie Corey would like to speak with you. Line two."

Joyce thought like an investigator. She was a former school teacher and mother whose youngest offspring had just graduated from high school. Her interruption against orders not to disturb me constituted a good decision. Joyce knew a phone call from Jackie Corey might once again trigger a major investigation.

Jackie was involved with the St. Louis chapter of one of the largest nonprofit child-help organizations in the Midwest. I had contacted her a year earlier, volunteering our services to help locate missing children, specifically ones who might be out of the country. Within a few months, Allied Intelligence answered an SOS from Jackie and engineered a danger-fraught recovery of two siblings—one in Mexico, the other in Peru— held by a sinister "religious" cult known as the Children of God.

I had no inkling when I picked up the phone to talk with this petite, intense, dedicated woman that the previous trek through Central American jungles would resemble a relaxed walk in the park compared with the difficulties lurking just ahead.

"How are you, Mike?"

"Fine," I said, rather businesslike, out of respect for her total commitment to a bulging caseload that permitted little time to dally with pleasantries. It staggers the imagination, the number of children who run away, or are hidden, kidnapped, or murdered. It literally amounts to a plague.

"Mike, do you have any experience in the Far East?"

"Yes." As a matter of fact, I had just returned from that part of the world, working the executive protection part of our business. I had been in Malaysia, Singapore, Japan, and Thailand.

"An agency for missing children in Washington, D.C., heard about your success with the Central American case and would like to refer a woman to you. She's trying to recover her four children, who likely are being held in Thailand."

"Give me some details, Jackie."

"It's bad. Of course, all cult cases are bad, but this one is infinitely more complicated because the kids are halfway around the world. The legal problems alone make the prospects very discouraging."

"What's the mother's name?"

"Vivian Shillander. She lives in Sioux Falls, South Dakota, and she's very upset, very emotional, as you can well understand."

From the worried, anxious tone of Jackie Corey's cracking voice I sensed there was more to this case than a routine cult kidnapping.

"What else, Jackie? Is there something you haven't told me?"

"Mike," she said, and I didn't think the tears I pictured in her eyes were imaginary, "we're dealing with the Children of God again. As incredible as it seems, these children are also trapped in that cult. Because of this, I knew you were the person for the job. Will you take it?"

"Probably, but first I need to talk with the mother. Have Mrs. Shillander call me."

"I will," Jackie said, hesitant to break off the conversation.

"We'll do what we can," I said.

"I suppose. It's just . . . that group is so . . . sickening. And evil. I'd prefer it to be almost anyone else."

"I know."

"I realize the case will be dangerous. I'm sorry."

"I haven't taken the case yet."

But she figured I would. "Well, Mike," Jackie said, "I guess it's 'here we go again.'"

She was referring to the recovery of those two children from Mexico and Peru. The route traveled in that case had been bumpy and torturous, but the end, despite long odds, had been a happy one.

I couldn't help fantasizing about what lay ahead this time. As I put down the phone and ignored the paperwork on my desk, my mind automatically played back what research and firsthand experience had taught me about Moses David Berg and the Children of God (COG), a religious cult founded in California in 1968, now operating in eighty countries with ten thousand members.

Youngsters—whether born into the Children of God or recruited by the cult—often underwent separation from their parents, placement in harsh, spartan communes, and nonstop brainwashing that aimed to achieve total submission to the aims of Moses David Berg.

COG ranks among the worst of the worst in a galaxy of bizarre "religious" cults that range from the pathetic and farcical to the murderous. Most Children of God members exist in extreme poverty while their super-rich leader wallows in the trappings of extravagant luxury. The phenomenal growth of Moses David Berg's cult can in part be traced to his doctrine of Flirty Fishing, whereby women members engage in "prostitution for Jesus," swelling Berg's coffers and increasing the cult's membership: The women attempt to recruit those they sleep with.

In 1979, Berg wrote in his statistical newsletter: "Our dear FF'ers are still going strong, God Bless'm, having now witnessed to over a quarter-of-a-million souls, loved over 25,000 of them and won nearly 19,000 to the Lord, along with about 35,000 new friends."*

In an interview reported in *Christianity Today* (2/18/77) former Children of God member David Jacks explained how even small children raise money for Moses David Berg:

> Kids go out on the streets for six to ten hours a day. In the States they bring in from $25 to $100 a day each. On the basis of ten people, that would mean $500 to $1,000 a day per colony, or $2,500 to $5,000 per week. This income is almost pure profit.

Berg, who claims Jesus Christ visits him, says his body is often possessed of people from the past, who then offer him counsel: Rasputin, the Pied Piper, Joan of Arc, Oliver Cromwell, Merlin the Magician, William Jennings Bryan, Martin Luther, and many more.

People make a big mistake if they dismiss Berg as a clownish crackpot. Said former Children of God cultist Jack Wasson in the same *Christianity Today* interview:

> Obviously, comparing himself to King David and Moses serves very nicely for his pyramid type of leadership structure, with penalties for disobedience of God's endtime leader. If your leader is wrong, God will judge him; but you must obey your leader.
>
> There was a case in Los Angeles in the early days when Abraham (an early COG leader) was giving a class on obeying leadership, and this illustration was used: "If your leader has told you to stand on a corner and witness, and a truck came bearing down on you, in that case you *might* be able to move. Otherwise, it your duty to *obey*, period." The result of this sort of indoctrination is a reign of terror. If you even question in your mind Moses' leadership, God will know it and you will be judged.

Rich individuals, including an English millionaire and an Italian duke, have loaned large sums of money to Berg, plus land

---

*Editor's Note: The COG claims it has since discontinued the practice of FF, in part because of the AIDS epidemic.

and homes for his cult followers to use. Of course, those recruited by the Children of God *turn over all their possessions.*

Muammar al-Qaddafi invited Berg to Libya in 1975, as the
"prophet's" daughter, Deborah Davis, later explained:

> Dad spent about a month in Libya. He had taken with
> him a troupe of girls and started an FF ministry among some
> military leaders and Qaddafi's personal staff. But Qaddafi was
> not interested in prostitution—the Koran forbids it—even
> though his officers were. Rather, the Libyan wanted only to
> make use of the ten thousand COG disciples who were dis-
> tributing literature around the world. Certainly we repre-
> sented an efficient means of promoting Qaddafi's Third
> International Theory.

Thirty minutes after talking with Jackie Corey, my office
door burst open and Joyce Henderson, eschewing the intercom,
said, "Vivian Shillander is calling from South Dakota." Joyce
grinned, caught up in the excitement of a possible international
child recovery operation.

It is remarkable how much attention a case involving children can stir up; people—whether working on or watching
it—get grabbed by the heart. It was no different during my
years with the Berkeley Police Department in St. Louis. Everyone, from the dispatcher to the most hard-bitten narcotics and
homicide detectives, myself included, made that extra push for
the sake of kids.

"This is Mike Intravia," I said.

"Hello. My name is Vivian Shillander. I've been trying to
locate someone like you for a long time. I finally obtained your
name from Jackie Corey. You recovered the Richert children
from Peru and Mexico, didn't you?"

Vivian had read accounts about the rescue, but the name
of our company hadn't been mentioned in the media coverage.

"Yes. We brought them home."

"Oh, Mr. Intravia, I hope you can help me, too," she said in
the quivering, sob-filled voice of every woman stricken with
fear for her children's safety.

"Jackie tells me you have four children who are still in the
COG."

"Yes. I was forced to leave them in Asia with their father. It's just terrible when I think of what's happening to them, and believe me, I know. We need to get them away from Richard and that organization. I've been trying everything, but so far . . ." Her voice broke off in a sob.

"Richard is your husband?"

"Yes."

"I assume he's still in COG."

"Oh, yes. He'll always be in COG."

"Mrs. Shillander . . . Vivian," I said, sensing a personal approach was needed for this distraught, tearful, right-on-the-edge mother. "I know it's hard, but please try to pull yourself together. I'll need a lot of help from you."

"All right. Yes. I'm sorry."

"If we're going to get your children back to the States, you'll have to provide me with background information. Let's start from the beginning; in this case, from when you first met Richard."

I waited while she collected her thoughts. Through hundreds of police and private investigation interviews, I had learned to remain silent and allow people whatever emotional response brought comfort. Telling someone "I know how you feel" does no good. Unless the detective has lived through the same agony, he or she *cannot* understand how someone else feels, *cannot* appreciate the pain, and shouldn't pretend otherwise, especially when children are involved.

Suddenly the story poured out of Vivian, like long pent-up water crashing through a broken dam.

Vivian, the daughter of a respected Methodist minister, related through her tears how she had met the Children of God and her future husband in 1971 in San Francisco. This was the era of the Vietnam War and protests against it. Many young people were "dropping out," or searching for what they called "alternative lifestyles." Unfortunately, Vivian found one of the worst.

"Richard and I witnessed for Jesus on the West Coast," she said. "I was eighteen at the time. After a year in California, we received orders from Moses David Berg to take his message abroad. What he taught wasn't anything like it is today. I still feel that early on the teachings were good, but a few years later they became perverse and radically contrary to what the Lord wants us to do."

Thus began the couple's odyssey across South America, Belgium, Italy, France, and, finally, the Far East. Along the way their marriage produced five children: John, now thirteen years old; April, eleven; Caleb, ten; Francisco, nine; and Yancha, three and a half.

At six-feet-four and 230 pounds, Richard, a high school dropout, had become a leader in the cult. Richard was committed to the teachings of Moses Berg. Each day he sent his four oldest out to "witness," Vivian said.

Gradually—over many years, for the cult's hold was strong—Vivian began to question her family's actions. She agonized long and hard, often crying herself to sleep, where nightmares waited.

Finally, she announced her intention to leave Thailand with her five children and return to the United States. Instead of sending her stateside, the cult locked her in a ten-by-ten-foot windowless room for thirty days to "think on your heresy and repent."

Vivian didn't repent. Instead she grew stronger in her conviction that along the present path resided disaster for her children. Cult members thereupon drove her and Yancha, then three months old and nursing, to the Bangkok airport and put them on a plane to California. Under no circumstances would they let her take the other four children, who were young and already committed to Moses David Berg, with a lifetime of enriching the prophet ahead of them.

Heartbroken, brainwashed, with no energy to fight a monolithic foe, the disillusioned cult outcast found her way back to South Dakota, where she had grown up. She returned as a stranger: Her minister father had died, and a fifteen-year absence had scattered her childhood friends.

For three and a half years in Sioux Falls, Vivian struggled to purge her mind of the cult's damaging influence and piece her life back together, an excruciating task made more difficult by haunting worry about the terrible present, and even worse future her four other children faced. During this period she largely stayed to herself, occasionally grasping at straws and flailing about helplessly, searching for a way to recover her children. As her vision became less clouded by tears, her mind less fogged by brainwashing, she ultimately managed to transform part of the cancerous sadness to anger, to strength, and finally to action.

Vivian joined the First Baptist Church of Sioux Falls, whose pastor, the Reverend Charles Landon, gently and cautiously managed to draw the moving story out of her. Determined to alleviate her predicament, Landon solicited donations from church members (who virtually adopted Vivian and her family), held prayer meetings to raise funds for a rescue effort, and in a key move, reached out to U.S. Senator Larry Pressler. The efforts of Landon and Pressler finally resulted in Jackie Corey's call to me.

Listening to Vivian recall her ordeal through sobs that could move the hardest heart, I knew this would be a tough investigation. I would have to hold a tight rein on *my* emotions and make decisions based strictly on logic, not anger. From my previous battle with the Children of God, I had a vivid, revolting picture of the wretched existence the Shillander children endured in the cult.

"Vivian, I understand the children are still in Thailand," I began.

"I'm not sure. You know how often COG moves, mainly to stay a jump ahead of the police and others who are looking for them. I think they're in Thailand, but they could have moved to Burma or Malaysia. I have an old address in Bangkok, but I doubt if it's any good now."

"It's a place to start."

"Do you think you can bring my children back?" Desperation tinged every word of Vivian's ultimate important question to me.

It's absolutely essential to be honest with clients. Raising false hope always comes back to haunt and embitter. A promise made today, even with the best intentions—to raise spirits that badly need lifting—can lead to terrible heartbreak down the line.

"I can't guarantee success," I said, "but I'll do the very

best job I can. No one has much experience recovering children from overseas, but I have more than most."

"Then you'll take the case?"

"Yes. But I can't do it alone. I'll need assistance from contacts, both here and abroad. Most important, I'll need your cooperation with whatever requests I make."

"Of course."

"Your commitment must be total, Vivian. I warn you: Don't pursue this unless you're prepared to travel a long, difficult road."

"I don't care what I have to do," she said with a determination and fierceness I had hoped to hear. Surely Vivian owned a deep reserve of resolve, strength, and courage. It had surfaced spectacularly in Bangkok when she had stood up to those stern COG leaders, all of them male, and decided to leave the only life she had known as an adult. I had wondered if that agonizing interim in Sioux Falls, necessary for healing, had also drained some of her inner resources. Maybe not, thanks to the love and concern of Charles Landon and those good Sioux Falls parishioners who had made her cause theirs.

"Know this for sure," I said, not wanting to repeat myself, but needing to be certain she understood what waited: "You're going to be severely tested."

"Mr. Intravia . . ."

"Mike." We were the same age, thirty-six.

"Mike, nothing can be worse than the loneliness and fear I've lived with since being separated from my children. I'm empty inside, wrung out, and I can't see going on without them. I'd gladly walk over burning coals if it would help. Surely you understand, talking to me, that I'm an emotional wreck, but there's nothing for any of us—not the kids, not me—if I don't get them back. I haven't any idea what I'm supposed to do, so I've decided to trust somebody completely, and that somebody is you."

What I said next wasn't prescient, but came from experience of what can go wrong when the explosive mix includes a bereft mother, brainwashed and programmed children, a father dedicated to a cult, and a determined, ruthless religious sect.

"Vivian, I'm glad you have this trust in me now, but the day will come when you won't, and that's when I'll want you to remember this talk. That's when I'll need your trust. I'm not being dramatic when I tell you it could be a matter of life and death."

It was time to lighten up. "Let's first worry about finding them," I said. "Maybe it won't be so tough. We're on the side of the angels, you know."

2

Weighing the Odds

I SPENT THE REST OF THAT June day thinking, planning, and discussing how to proceed with the case. I would have much preferred action, a break-down-the-door frontal assault on whatever dismal structure Richard stored the children in (no nice house for COG members—that would eat away profits from Berg's bottom-line balance sheet). Assuming I found the children, a doubtful prospect, I could end up in an Asian jail if I charged Rambo-style into a foreign country violating local laws left and right. COG had both money and influence; I knew the cult had gotten close to important Libyans, plus at least one powerful Thai military figure.

Vivian Shillander had called me her "last hope," a position I was neither comfortable with, wanted, nor found helpful. I didn't want to be anybody's "last hope," and the added pressure of such a designation wouldn't improve job performance even a little bit.

Besides, not all cases are solvable, and I had to wonder if my contacts in Thailand were capable of assisting with a child recovery. In the past I'd used these people in conjunction with the protective services Allied Intelligence provides worldwide, not for anything remotely resembling a rescue.

Even with crackerjack assistance from Thailand, we faced a cunning, formidable opponent in the Children of God. The cult routinely resorted to Machiavellian tactics to conceal the whereabouts of its members. And if alerted to our mission, if we made a mistake or just got unlucky and the COG found out about us, they would take Vivian's children so far underground in another Third World country she might never see them again.

COG members live in jungles, communes, refugee camps—any place affording cheap housing—to keep expenses low and tribute to Moses David Berg high. A detective trying to track down a cult member likely won't benefit from standard information, such as the individual's name or last known address, i.e., Joe Blow, 932 Mockingbird Lane. First of all, a lean-to shack built on a nameless pig trail doesn't have a house number; and secondly, many of these people assume unregistered, untraceable aliases, usually Old Testament biblical names.

By obeying Berg's mandates for austerity and freedom from worldly encumbrances, an entire band of his nomadic disciples can pick up and move within thirty minutes, less time than an average American family of four needs to pack the station wagon for a weekend camping trip. Even in the normal course of events, COG members typically move every couple of months. We could wind up playing an open-ended game of hide-and-seek.

The more I thought, the more obstacles I perceived, and it took a second to realize that Scott Biondo had entered the room and stood beside my desk, his lips curled into an eager smile.

Scott, just twenty-six, but already with five years in the business, was one of Allied Intelligence's youngest detectives, and one of the best. Aggressive and resourceful, he was extremely brave. Scott's friends likened this very eligible bachelor to James Bond because of his handsome features and the intrigue associated with the many international cases he had worked. To me, Scott's most important attributes are his steadfast loyalty and trustworthiness.

He stood in front of my desk, his expression serious. "I heard," he said.

"Heard what?"

"Come on. It's a big case, isn't it?"

"Maybe. What do you want?"

"To work on the investigation. It's a child recovery in the Far East, right?"

"Yes, and one that will be very dangerous." I didn't expect this to deter him, and it didn't.

"I enjoy that kind," he said. It was true—and not a bad attitude to have. Discretion and caution, which Scott possessed in abundance, were good qualities to have, but the sine qua non for an investigator was being able to handle risk, even to like it.

"I'll think it over," I said, "after I see how the case takes shape."

"Okay," he said, heading back to his office, "I just wanted to toss my hat in the ring early."

Normally I would seek an individual much more experienced than Scott. However, I knew this might be a case where youth, enthusiasm, and aggressiveness outranked investigative skills. I could choose a more seasoned detective, but not one more zealous. Besides, Scott had recently returned from an assignment with me in Southeast Asia, and had met some of the agency's contacts in Thailand. But it was too early in the program. I decided not to decide.

I hit the intercom button: "Don, when you get a minute, I have something to tell you."

Don Kissell and I had worked many cases together back when I was with the Berkeley Police Department in St. Louis. We became friends, as partners tend to do, and formed Allied Intelligence while still on the force. I also took a position as director of corporate security for a hotel chain.

Our company flourished, thanks largely to contacts developed while working at the hotels, and when we broke into international protection and overseas investigations, I gambled and became a full-time private investigator, a move which paid off for both of us.

Don Kissell is a devoted, caring, streetwise detective with standout people skills who proved every day that nice guys can be tough. Fellow Berkeley officers joked that criminals waited in line to confess to Don, and he acquired the nickname Father Don. He was my partner and good friend, and we survived several life-threatening situations together because we worked as a true team.

I gave him what few details I had about the case, and we discussed our past experiences with the Children of God. When we finished he said, "Don't forget to pack your camouflage fatigues. You'll want to be fashionable in the jungle."

I bowed and walked into the dojo that evening. All my advanced students were dressed in full traditional black karate gis. I had changed prior to coming to class and wore my instructor's uniform with black belt tied and hanging from my waist.

The students bowed respectfully, then shook my hand. I am a second-degree black belt in Kajukenbo Karate, a martial art emphasizing street-applicable self-defense. I have studied martial arts for twenty of my thirty-six years, making it a way of life.

As we loosened up before our workout, I couldn't push thoughts of the new case out of my mind. One of my brown belt advanced students, my younger brother Joe, approached and asked, "Is something wrong?"

"No," I said.

"You look very uptight tonight."

"It's nothing," I said and clapped my hands, signaling the students to line up for class.

We had an extra hard, painful workout, and I inadvertently pushed the students to the limit. I found myself using them for practice as much as instruction, and they kept picking themselves up off the floor.

When class ended, everyone bowed, and once again paid their respect. Joe came up as I was packing the equipment. "Sifu," he said, using the traditional name for addressing a black belt, "you started an important case today, didn't you?"

"What makes you say that?"

"Every time you beat the stuffing out of us, you've usually taken on another kidnapping."

I continued packing my gear, but Joe wouldn't quit until he found out. Seven years my junior, he'd always shown a keen interest in the business.

Joe is a talented mechanic who spent the first years of his adult life touring the country on a motorcycle. His unwavering dedication to me and to martial arts has brought us closer than most brothers.

"You're right about the new case, Joe," I said. "I didn't realize it was so obvious."

"Can you tell me what it's about, or is it confidential?"

"Another child recovery from a cult, only this time it's on the other side of the world."

Joe laughed and asked, "Have you told Patti?"

"Not yet. I will tonight." Even as a policeman and detective in St. Louis, I had wondered what good was accomplished by sharing descriptions of my work life with my wife. It created anxiety and stress, and not just for her. I worried because she did.

We had been married fifteen years, and not long after becoming a police officer in 1978, I determined it best to keep family life separate from work. How was Patti enriched by knowing I searched for a wife-beater who clubbed his spouse to death with a baseball bat? Or a rapist of children? Or a savage gas-station stickup "artist" who shot and killed two attendants because he didn't want to leave any witnesses?

Gory stories of patrolling mean streets couldn't lend her serenity, nor could depictions of dreary courtrooms, depressing jail cells, and cold morgues. She didn't meet the people I dealt with—muggers, maniacs, murderers, misfits turned callous and vicious by conditions sociologists, not cops, are supposed to understand—and I didn't think she was poorer for not knowing about them.

Like many cops, I needed to live two lives, keep them separate, be very careful not to permit overlap. I had to guard against behaving at home like I sometimes did on the street, where television news programs and police melodramas never catch the sad reality of filth, loss, degradation, and hopelessness: a coroner's slab where they cut corpses from crotch to throat; kids screaming over a dead mother's body; parents, too old to grow any more children, gazing blankly at their last hope, faded and cold; a young woman suddenly become a widow; or a trembling cocaine baby now an orphan.

What gain for Patti to learn these things?

But she knew anyway, and now I'd have to tell her about Thailand and the Children of God. However, I would share with her only basic details about the case. Sensitive and intelligent, she would realize that a Third World country such as Thailand could make the most dangerous St. Louis streets seem like dinner on the grounds at a country church.

My daughters Tanya and Erica greeted me with hugs and kisses when I came in the front door. Ages eleven and eight, they had been taking dance lessons at the Performing Arts Center, becoming quite serious students, and on that early evening they sat me down to watch their newest ballet moves.

Watching Tanya and Erica dance made me realize, not for the first time, how fast time passes. I tried to remember where I had been the last year, and what possibly could have been so important, that I had missed this remarkable development of skill and grace.

"What do you think of your ballerinas?" Patti asked as she came into the room, dressed in a pretty red sundress. She sat next to me on the couch. "You're still sweaty; it must have been a good session tonight."

"What did you think, Dad?" Erica asked.

"Beautiful. I didn't know you could dance as gracefully as I do."

"Dad! I could just see you in a tutu."

"You both look great. I can't wait to catch your recital."

"Dinner is ready when you clean up," Patti said.

"I've got something to tell you," I said to her after our daughters had gone downstairs.

"What is it?"

"I took a child recovery case," I said, hesitating.

"Do you have any idea where the child is?"

"Children. Four of them. All from the same family. I have some leads, but you know how these cases go. A month or even a year from now, the location may have changed several times."

"Mike . . ."

"I'll probably have to go to Thailand," I blurted out, to get the worst part over with.

"Thailand! They kill people for fifty dollars in Thailand! Tell me you're kidding."

"I'm not kidding. We've got a mother who hasn't seen her children for four years, and they're in that sick damn cult."

"The Children of God?"

"Yes. Probably in a jungle refugee camp, living under the perverted laws of that screwball Moses David Berg."

"My God!" Patti said. "Well, I'm glad you're going to try and find them. Do what you can for the mother, whoever she is. It breaks my heart to think about children in that horrible cult. Begging for money to give to their leaders. Living in communes and refugee camps. Oh, Mike, I think of Erica and Tanya, and say it couldn't happen to them, but I know it could."

She got up from the couch and began to pace. "Tell me about the mother," she said.

So I related what I knew of Vivian Shillander's story, and added, "She had a lot of courage to stand up to her overbearing husband and those other Children of God leaders, who are walking definitions of male chauvinism."

"That poor woman," Patti said. "I don't know how she takes it. I don't know whether I could, if the cult had our children. Mike, you've got to come through for her. You know that, don't you?"

During the night I thought about Patti—no way to conceal information from her about this case. And Vivian Shillander, so far just a distraught voice on the phone, crying out for her own flesh and blood, the issues of her womb. And the four helpless children, living from pillar to post with no hope of securing a stable home environment, trapped in a too real nightmare.

Patti had been right: I must succeed in this investigation. I could only hope I'd be good enough, and lucky enough.

Had a computer researcher handicapped my chances, I suppose his data entry would have started with the following biographical information:

NAME: Michael Serfino Intravia

HEIGHT: 6 feet

WEIGHT: 185 pounds

HAIR: light brown

EYES: blue

BIRTH SIGN: Virgo

GRADE SCHOOL: St. Kevin Catholic Grade School, St. Louis, Missouri

HIGH SCHOOL: Ritenour High School, St. Louis, Missouri.

COLLEGE: Associate degree in criminal justice and bachelor's degree in psychology and criminal justice, Northeast Missouri State University

SPECIALIZED TRAINING: Greater St. Louis Police Academy;
                         advance certification in electronic
                         countermeasures; safety and security
                         training; FBI course on hostage
                         negotiation; crime scene photo-
                         graphy; crime scene processing;
                         investigative techniques; executive
                         protection; international executive
                         protection; rape and homicide inves-
                         tigation; expert qualified with a
                         handgun, and numerous other
                         weapons.

The computer researcher also would have programmed my martial arts experience into the equation. It began in 1969 when I walked inside a St. Louis karate academy where I had often watched classes through the window. Its name was Black Belt Karate School, located in St. Ann, where I grew up, and the teacher was Walt Bone.

I wasn't old enough to drive, and had ridden my bicycle there daily. I talked with the teacher about the cost of lessons and he told me to bring my parents in.

Mom and Dad didn't want me studying karate, and refused to sign me up. They did agree, however, that if I could find a way to earn the money to pay my own way, they would allow me to attend.

I talked with Mr. Bone and pleaded with him to let me clean the school, or do odd jobs to pay my tuition.

To Walt Bone a student's desire was more important than money. So I began by paying what I could and cleaning the dojo.

I studied Tae Kwon Do under him for several years before entering the military, and continued my lessons in California, where I was first stationed, learning a style called Kenpo Karate.

In 1972, after a transfer to Honolulu, Hawaii, I joined a large Tae Kwon Do school on the northern part of the island. The school was so big it had numerous teachers; one of them was Kyo Lee, to whom I was assigned. The school's teachings, I soon learned, had strayed from traditional martial arts and become an uncoordinated street-fighting class.

A Korean martial arts purist, Kyo Lee broke away from the school and invited his students to join him, which I did. As a brown belt, I became one of his assistant instructors.

One day five cars pulled up in front of the school and fifteen men got out, dressed in white gis with brown or black belts tied around their waists.

The master walked in front, with his students and other black belts in tow. Kyo Lee stopped his class. Silence hung eerily in the air, along with the unmistakable quiet-before-a-storm aura of impending catastrophe.

We were asked by the old master to come with him and abandon Kyo Lee. He particularly addressed me, saying I was *his* student. After I refused, the master suggested one of his students fight me in a skills comparison.

Kyo Lee nodded for me to step forward and meet the challenge. The fight began. I was under the impression it would be a controlled martial arts bout, but after several barefoot, full-contact punches in the mouth, and the loss of a half-pint of blood, I knew it was no mere contest. I fought to survive, rather than to win, and a minute later my opponent lay on the ground bleeding and unable to return to his feet.

The master clapped his hands, and his students attacked. The scene resembled a particularly violent Chinese karate movie, except this one was played out in deadly earnest.

Kyo Lee shouted for the battle to cease, and it did, momentarily. He approached the other master and challenged *him* to fight, rather than the students.

The master agreed and assumed a fighting stance. Kyo Lee, already in his pose, said something in Korean, then in English, making clear the challenge would be to the death. No one doubted the depth of his commitment.

The old master came out of his fighting stance slowly, not wanting to startle Kyo Lee. He backed off without saying another word, and signaled his students to return to their vehicles.

From that day forward martial arts became a way of life, and I developed a desire for hard, serious training, rather than working out for fun, relaxation, and exercise.

In 1974, just as I prepared to test for my black belt under Kyo Lee, I was transferred back to St. Louis. I drifted for nine years, working out on my own, and studied a few other martial arts regimens until January 1983, when I finally found a new teacher, Sifu Doug Washburn.

I quickly covered the basics and began advanced teachings of Kajukenbo, ironically, a style which originated in the Hawaiian Islands. Kajukenbo, extremely rigid, placed strong emphasis on practical defense.

These intense classes usually generated some form of injury—from bloody noses to deep bruises—but I ate them up like candy. Most friends thought my training was too strenuous, a killing regimen, and to a certain degree they were correct. Surely the program was meant for only a few.

On July 28, 1985, I received my black belt after surviving a test that left me with raw and broken knuckles, a displaced rib, weight five pounds less than when I started, and a deep sense of pride in having survived.

I taught karate classes for the city recreation departments in St. Charles and O'Fallon for awhile and currently operate my own school, the Midwest School of Martial Arts, near historic Lindenwood College in St. Charles. I require the hard, traditional style of karate training for black and brown belt students, and in the past four years only two out of hundreds have evinced the desire to train for these ranks. One of them is my brother Joe.

That computer handicapper of my chances would also have learned that even as a child I wanted to become a detective. I never tired of playing spy and detective games that to me were not games.

Before leaving the military I took a part-time job as a store detective for Sears, and became friends with several police detectives who had positions I envied. In 1978, I was hired by the Berkeley Police Department in St. Louis, and examiners asked what my aspirations were for five years down the road. I said without hesitation, I wanted to be a detective. I reached that goal three years early, becoming at age twenty-eight one of the youngest detectives in the city.

Frankly, I loved the job. The danger appealed to me, along with the daily challenge of putting myself on the line, but more important I felt I made a difference. Countless crimes never got committed because I had helped take the felon off the street.

Allied Intelligence has become a highly successful business operating in numerous foreign countries with many major corporate clients, but occasionally I get the itch to shelve it all, to ask for my badge back, and be a cop again.

As it turned out, I remained in police work until 1985 (I cofounded Allied in 1980, moonlighting for almost six years), investigating everything from auto theft to robbery, burglary, embezzlement, rape, and murder. The area of the city I worked—near the St. Louis airport, Lambert Field—had depressed many, but not me. I never lost enthusiasm for my childhood dream.

So what were the odds? I wondered. Not good, when measured by the ten-thousand-mile distance, and the numerous other negatives: little money for investigation, no idea where the children were kept, hostile Asian laws, and a resourceful, well-organized opponent.

But the odds were in my favor, I believed, if commitment and effort determined the outcome. I wondered if that imaginary computer could calculate determination.

▲
Area near where
the children were
recovered.

3

Only One Chance

THE NEXT MORNING, June 23, 1987, I logged #AI87–0170 into the books and began the investigation. I spent the first hours developing a lead sheet, paperwork detailing an organized approach to the case.

We faced many negatives, chief among them the possibility of COG discovering that we were searching for the children. If that happened, I strongly suspected Vivian would never see her children again. I had to operate on the belief that at best we would have one chance at recovery, and one chance only.

If COG or Richard found out we were coming for the children, they would *immediately* exit whatever country they resided in through an uncontrolled checkpoint, and vanish into a remote jungle in another part of the world.

Their location would remain protected, and they would move regularly for several years. By then the children would be hopelessly brainwashed adults, virtual robots, their minds filled with trash—puppets activated by the string-pulling master manipulator, Moses David Berg. It behooved us, needless to say, to operate as covertly as possible.

I reviewed what I knew about Richard Shillander, white male; date of birth, November 21, 1952; height, 6'4"; weight, 230 pounds; dark brown hair; brown eyes; slightly bucked teeth; noticeably squared chin with dimple in the center.

This slogan-muttering man, utterly committed to the dogma of Moses David Berg, had ruled his family with the heaviest of hands. I knew he would do anything in his power to please his superiors in the cult. The young, after all, had a life-time of earning potential ahead of them.

Most slaves had it better. Generally they were not forced to mouth paeans to their oppressor.

Vivian had described her husband as possessing a certain cunning intelligence—a cut above that of a wolf, I thought—which positioned him higher in the COG pecking order than the foot-soldier women and children. She deemed him a formidable adversary, a cult leader who would be hard to find. Even more difficult would be the challenge of taking the children away from him.

Everything had to be accomplished legally. I wouldn't work any other way, and staying within the bounds of the law represented the client's best interest as well. If the children were recovered with the methods a mercenary might employ, people might get hurt, and Vivian could end up looking bad.

Also, self-interest dictated abiding by established rules. My reputation could suffer irreparable damage if we cowboyed it in Asia. The large, conservative corporations we represent did not want to read about, and risk being associated with, a chaos-creating loose cannon gone amok in some small Third World nation. He would win kudos from tabloids and television sleaze shows, but frowns—or worse—from the more respected and thoughtful mainstream media.

No matter what country we found the children in, we needed to walk a thin line. Vivian had to obtain first-rate legal advice, because without court-assigned custody of the children, no country—not even the United States—would provide any assistance.

Before taking any steps on foreign soil, we had to have more than just a *suspicion* that the children lived there. If the offspring were held in Thailand, the Thai Embassy in the United States had to be persuaded to certify Vivian's custody documents before she could take possession of her children.

Clients usually become extremely discouraged and disillu-sioned when they seek assistance from the U.S. government in these areas. There are departments that have been established at federal levels whose red tape can be maddening. Many peo-ple dead-end at this point, unless they have professional experi-ence in working with the federal system.

Foreign contacts are the key to a successful overseas investigation. Even Sherlock Holmes would founder if he didn't know the customs, laws, people, and language of the nation where he worked.

Having just completed an assignment in the Far East, I didn't qualify as a total stranger, and with difficulty I could even make myself understood in Thai. Also, I had previously nurtured a relationship with the American Embassy there, and with an influential investigator. This latter would be heavily relied on.

In fact, for a young company specializing in corporate protection, we had done quite a bit of globe-trotting: France, West Germany, Austria, Malaysia, Japan, Brazil, Argentina, Mexico, Paraguay, Colombia, Monaco, Canada, and a dozen other nations.

That first morning I wrote a letter to Vallop Kingchansilp, a private investigator in Bangkok:

> I have accepted a child recovery case which I believe will require some investigation in your country. I will have more details regarding this matter very soon and would be honored if you would assist me. The children are in a religious cult called the Children of God, a group you may already have information about.
>
> Please consider this investigation confidential. The Children of God would take immediate evasive action if they suspect an investigation is being conducted on any of them.
>
> I am looking forward to seeing you again, and hope we can work together on this matter.

I had confidence Vallop would stand ready to help in any way possible. Businessmen in Thailand are much more formal than in the United States, and Vallop would consider it an honor to him that I had requested his help; likewise, I should deem it an honor to have him accept the case. Actually, all this "honor" becomes more of a contract than any piece of paper Americans sign.

There are many cultural attitudes that make this part of the world one of my favorite places. Its friendly, polite people show great respect for one another, a concept coinciding with my martial arts training. In Thailand, a person's word is his honor, and honor is the most valued possession. Without honor, money and all material belongings are considered worthless. An individual's word is not questioned, and you must stand by your own.

Some people in our country feel the same way. My first day as a rookie policeman, Sergeant Tom Brown, a veteran cop who knew the streets better than anyone in the department, said, "From the first person you interact with as a police officer to the last, you must stand by what you promise. Bad guys know which officers to push and which ones to leave alone. If you tell an individual, 'do this or else,' always follow through; otherwise, your effectiveness will be diminished. Follow through on what you say, and never threaten something you can't back up."

Sergeant Brown's words paralleled the Oriental concept of honor.

I genuinely hoped the investigation would take me to Thailand. But I also had to consider Thailand's many next-door neighbors: Malaysia, Burma, Laos, Cambodia—and possibly China, where COG had a growing movement. Nevertheless, for the moment, I contacted only Vallop; Thailand represented the last known address for Richard and the children.

I considered contacting Washington, D.C. to check for activity on the passports of Vivian's family members. Somewhere in the labyrinth of official documentation regarding the comings and goings of American citizens sat a computer terminal which, with the push of a button, could trace the movements of Richard, John, April, Caleb, and Francisco Shillander. But bare handed, without the right cutting tool (a court document awarding Vivian custody of the children), I couldn't peel off even a strip of the red tape blocking the entrance to the intricate governmental maze that then would have to be traversed.

Vivian remained married to Richard, and no custody had been formally assigned. Down and out in Sioux Falls, with a baby to care for and her estranged husband on the other side of the world, Vivian hadn't filed for divorce. Although she now would have to go for all of it—divorce, custody, and recovery of the children—trying to explain the story to a Washington bureaucrat would be impossible. We needed temporary custody papers.

I called Vivian in South Dakota. "I need a few minutes to discuss your case," I said.

"I have all the time in the world."

"I'd like the name of your attorney."

It was Steve Haugaard. He practiced out of the Hanson Building in Sioux Falls.

I told Vivian the most pressing matter was to complete all the legal paperwork required to have a court grant her custody of the children.

Haugaard had already worked on it, she said, but how fast she didn't know. I asked Vivian to have him call me. I knew few attorneys had experience with this type of case, and maybe I could help, or direct him to someone who could.

"Vivian," I said, "I'd also like you to contact Senator Pressler's office again. Keep your case in front of him, right on the front burner. It could help us tremendously somewhere down the line."

We talked more about her own ordeal, and the help she had received from people in Sioux Falls once her story became known.

"I couldn't have gotten this far by myself," she said. "And it wasn't until I joined First Baptist that I found the strength and support I needed to make the decision to proceed."

She described the kind personal interest Pastor Chuck Landon and other members of the First Baptist Church evinced in helping her. One of those parishioners, Brad Beckstrom, served on Senator Pressler's staff.

"I have a lot of people who are cheering for me," Vivian said. "God bless them, but none of them have any experience with this kind of situation."

I obtained the names and birth dates of the four children held by COG:

Mahaleel John Shillander: 11/10/74

April May Shillander: 4/3/76

Caleb David Shillander: 9/7/77

Francisco Javier (Tito) Shillander: 2/13/79

"Tito was born in Valencia, Spain," Vivian said, fighting off tears. So many tears.

"You just stay strong," I said. "And stay on top of your attorney. Have him resolve that custody question. Without custody, nobody will give us the time of day."

Later that morning I pulled out the April Richert file. In 1986, we had worked for April, tracking and recovering her son and daughter from the Children of God.

April lives in St. Louis and, like Vivian, had joined COG with her husband. While in the cult she gave birth to four children.

The doctrine of Flirty Fishing and other sexual teachings finally drove her out of COG, and she brought her four children home. Shortly afterward her husband, Mark, "renounced" the cult and came to St. Louis to see his offspring.

Mark Richert hung around for a couple of weeks before cult members came through town and persuaded him to rejoin the COG fold. Mark took the two oldest, Sebastian and Christina, for a visit. When he didn't return them, April began checking, and discovered her now-former-husband had packed and apparently left the state. Despite papers granting legal custody of the children, April had no luck obtaining police or FBI assistance. She hired private investigators, who were unsuccessful, and finally came to us through a referral from Jackie Corey.

I met with April and promised we would do everything possible to recover her missing children. A caring, concerned, loving mother, April personified the type of wronged parent it required a heart of stone *not* to want to help.

Months of intense investigation led us from one country to another, until we received a definitive tip that Mark Richert resided in Mexico. Ultimately we found Christina living in Mexico City, and filed charges that led to her father's arrest.

Mark Richert refused to cooperate, and the whereabouts of his son Sebastian remained unknown. Christina didn't have any idea as to her brother's location, but she did lead us to another COG house in Mexico City.

Cult members inside the residence, mistaking our taxi driver for a Mexican federal police official, cooperated to avoid conflict with government and law-enforcement authorities. The cult had been booted out of numerous nations, and Berg himself would have ratted if he thought the only alternative meant losing a territory currently safe for exploitation.

A day later Sebastian was returned from Lima, Peru, where he and some other twelve-year-olds were undergoing "training" and indoctrination into cult teachings. COG typically separates adolescents from their parents, shipping them off to what amounts to brainwashing camps. Isolated from family and friends, "divinely inspired" by the teachings of Berg, these young people become dependent on their "instructors," and they develop a syndrome not unlike that experienced by Middle East hostages kept for extended periods of time by their captors: The thinking of the captured becomes that of the captor.

Of course, no one at these brainwashing camps ever questions the teachings, which are drilled ceaselessly, rote style, into impressionable minds.

April Richert's story ended happily. The damage caused her children turned out to be reversible. Large doses of tender loving care enabled them to start life anew, with all the hopes and opportunities young people ought to have.

After reviewing the final page of the Richert file, I closed the folder, took a deep breath, and again made a pledge to do my best to provide the Shillander children with a fighting chance at having a normal life.

The summer boiled hot, typical for St. Louis. Nonetheless, I wouldn't trade my hometown for any other city on the planet. I have been fortunate to visit many of the most exotic, romantic, and exciting places in the world, and they are everything I imagined them to be.

I wouldn't describe St. Louis as exotic, romantic, or even exciting, though we have good schools, a fine symphony orchestra, excellent restaurants, spacious green parks, and the mighty Mississippi River. It's simply a good place to live and raise a family. St. Louisans are for the most part friendly and proud of their neighborhoods. And the city maintains a steadier economy than most. Of course, our two claims to international fame are the Gateway Arch, symbolizing the entry to the West, and our world-famous St. Louis Cardinals baseball team.

Still, heat counted as the one thing everyone shared in
the summer. Ferocious as it became, while we painstakingly
prepared the groundwork for a full-bore recovery effort in the
Far East, we knew it ranked as the most minor of discomforts
compared to what the children suffered. The "we" applied to
Vivian's case more than to any in which I had been associated.
Every investigator—and we had several dozen full- and part-
time—every secretary, even family members of investigators
and clerical personnel, never let a day pass without wondering
how the children fared.

Steve Haugaard called to introduce himself, and to ask
for any suggestions I might have to assist him in obtaining custody rights for Vivian. Steve confessed he had never tried to
settle a custody case involving a cult and out-of-the-country
complications.

I had to laugh. The number of attorneys with such experience likely numbered fewer than ten in the whole nation.

Allied Intelligence works with hundreds of attorneys,
many like Steve. Generally a lawyer advises us what he wants
and what he intends to accomplish. But most attorneys, like
doctors, operate a *general* practice, and for some cases must rely
on a specialist. A professional will acknowledge a lack of exper-
tise in a new field and seek out someone with experience. I
hardly qualified as a veteran of a thousand battles—no one
did—but I had at least traveled the route.

Haugaard impressed me as compassionate and thoroughly
devoted to Vivian's cause. A member of the First Baptist
Church in Sioux Falls, he said he considered it his Christian
duty to help however he could.

I related to Haugaard the channels April Richert had gone
through to obtain custody of her children, and advised him to
gather information on the impoverished lifestyle children suffer in the COG. I gave him the phone number of Dave Howard,
a St. Louis attorney who had traveled the twisted legal route for
April Richert. I knew Dave would help, having himself gotten a
bellyful of COG. Finally, I emphasized the need not only to
deal with the U.S. Embassy in Thailand, but also the Thai Embassy in the United States, which needed to certify all papers as
"official U.S. documents."

The perfect scenario entailed locating Richard and the children, and then retaining a Thai lawyer who could obtain a judgment in his country recognizing Vivian's custody rights.

I knew better than to be optimistic. Thailand features a totally male-dominated culture. The father, typically, exercises complete control over his family, and doesn't even have to recognize a divorce.

Steve Haugaard's complex process of piecing together the paperwork to gain legal custody for Vivian took time. While Vivian waited, trying to cope as best she could with lonely, empty days, time passed more quickly for me as I worked other cases, mainly those involving another one of our clients, Major League Baseball. Peter Ueberroth, the commissioner, had formed an investigative and legal task force to combat black market copyright infringement of trademarks of Major League Baseball souvenirs. We helped with that task.

Allied Intelligence also handled investigations for the St. Louis Cardinals, and the concentration was particularly heavy that year, with the Cardinals headed for the playoffs and the World Series.

When the World Series concluded, we had confiscated truckloads of counterfeit merchandise, eliminated illegal printing operations, and obtained numerous arrests. All this helped fill the days while we waited for Vivian to struggle her way through the American court system.

▲
Area near where
the children were
recovered.

◄ Courtyard area inside
the Guest House
grounds.

4

Retreat and Remembrance

FOR CASES AS INTENSE AND EMOTIONALLY charged as the search for the Shillander children, I had a retreat, a place to unwind, relax, and think.

When Patti and I hired a contractor to build our home in St. Charles, a west side St. Louis suburb, we agreed she would design and decorate everything, except for one room I reserved for myself: a twenty-four-by-twenty-foot section of the basement converted into a personal dojo, which to a serious martial artist is more than a workout studio; it is sacred and treated with great respect.

From the basement game room a visitor sees nothing unusual about the stained-wood, six-panel door leading to another room. Yet it opens to a space housing a special part of my life.

The smell alone provides a unique experience for most. Several Oriental liniments permeate the air with the heavy odor of musk. Hanging on the walls are many different weapons I train with and artifacts I have collected while traveling in the Orient.

One Saturday night in October, while still on hold with the Shillander case (Vallop, despite an impressive effort, had so far drawn a blank), I sought refuge from the tension of the wait in my dojo.

I began the workout by applying and carefully kneading liniments into various muscles. Then I deviated from the traditional regimen by pushing a button on my tape player. The first song, a favorite, "Highway to the Danger Zone," shifted my attitude into high gear, and I made the speed bag beat to the music. Later, as I was throwing kicks at the heavy bag, the door to the dojo creaked open. Scott Biondo had arrived.

Scott, my colleague at Allied Intelligence and one of my Kajukenbo students, wore a traditional karate uniform exactly like mine. As serious about martial arts training as he is about becoming a first-class international investigator, he is competitive in most areas of life, always striving to perform at the optimum level. I had been instructing Scott in both traditional martial arts and specific self-defense tactics necessary for survival in our line of work.

"Sifu," Scott said. He shook my hand.

"I'm glad you could make it tonight. Go ahead and loosen up."

We had a hard session, circuit training to the music, and concluding with knife-fighting tactics.

"That was good," he said. Each of us glistened with sweat.

"Scott, what does the smell in the dojo bring to mind?"

"An armpit?" he deadpanned.

"Try again."

"Other than sweat, the Oriental liniments remind me of places we visited in the Far East."

"You ready to breathe those odors again?"

"If you're talking about the Shillander case, you know I am."

"Well, I'm going to use you. But we need to talk."

"Now is a good time for me."

And right now, I believed, not unkindly, *you're ready to hop a jet for Thailand.*

Ten years ago, when I was Scott's age, I would have felt the same way.

"I've given this decision a lot of thought," I said. *Too much thought,* I almost blurted out, *and not enough action. Everything's far too cerebral.*

It couldn't be any other way, I knew, but that didn't help. It didn't help me, or Vivian. We both wanted me up and about, finding those kids, grabbing them, returning them to her.

All I *had* done, all I *could* do, was fire off letters and phone calls to Vallop, who each time had nothing to report. I knew he did his best—that he was one of the best—and I had to fight the urge to go to Thailand myself.

Right now I couldn't accomplish anything there, not in a country of 518,000 square miles and 50 million people. Few natives knew their homeland as well as Vallop knew his, and the hunt had totally frustrated him.

"This case," I said to Scott, "is different from any investigation we've worked, or likely ever will work. No matter how well we perform, we may fail."

"Mike, I'm not worried," he said cockily. "I'm confident we'll find those kids, no matter where they are, in Thailand, Malaysia, wherever, and bring them home."

"This is no macho, hopped-up adventure," I answered angrily. "I chose you for your enthusiasm and your guts, but I insist you follow instructions and not try to wing it. This case can be a great experience for you. You can learn a lot, *if* you take the time."

"I'll come through for you."

"I know you will; otherwise, I wouldn't have picked you," I said, then hesitated. "Besides, you made the decision easier for me."

"How so?"

"Everyone acted gung ho, but you were the only one dumb enough to volunteer."

It was indeed time to pursue the case more actively. Vivian searched through boxes of papers filled with scattered memories and came up with some leads:

- Her passport number, which alone would have been useless, except it had been obtained at the same time as Richard's. The numbers would be only one or two digits apart.
- Richard, the high school dropout, had worked at Queens High School in Thailand, teaching English. He had also taught advanced English to young Thai cadets at a military base.
- An address for Richard *and* another for the COG area leader.
- Richard's biblical name: "Barz," short for "Barzalli."

• The most recent pictures of the four children, which Vivian had received by mail from them in September 1984. The pictures were taken at a refugee camp meeting on the Thai-Cambodian border, and the children were surrounded by thousands of refugees.

The leads held promise, but they were several years old. I needed Richard's passport number and those of the children. With Vivian's number and everyone's date of birth, they might be obtainable. I called Senator Pressler's Sioux City office. The time had come to test his commitment to this cause.

"Mike. How are you doing?" Brad Beckstrom's friendly tone boded well when I called.

"I presume you remember me."

"Sure, I do. As a matter of fact, your name is mentioned almost on a daily basis at church. I don't know whether I told you that I'm a member of First Baptist in Sioux Falls, where Vivian belongs, and all of us are hoping you'll get those children out of that sick cult."

"That's why I'm calling. I need some information you may be able to obtain."

"I'll do whatever I can, Mike. Senator Pressler has authorized me to do everything possible to help."

"I need the passport numbers of Richard and the children; plus, I want to know if they have active visas for Thailand, or anywhere else. I will have Vivian call and make a formal request with your office for the information."

"I'll check. You know the red tape in government offices. It will probably take a while, but I'll move on it right away. And, Mike, I want you to know that everyone at church is praying for your success."

I felt comfortable with Brad, who seemed sincerely dedicated to this project. He was no two-faced politician throwing around cheap words. I had never visited Sioux Falls nor known anyone from there, but I imagined I would like the place and its people.

I flipped my Rolodex to Vallop's phone number. I had several leads for him to begin working, the sooner the better. Although the legal work Vivian needed was far from complete, I'd decided to get a few more of my own ducks in a row so we could move when Haugaard gave the word.

I dialed the area code for Bangkok, Thailand, then put down the phone when I remembered the fourteen-hour time difference. *Whoa, Mike,* I thought, reining in my eagerness. *Call from home at midnight.*

I really had acted too quickly and needed to recall techniques used previously when working with Thais. Americans generally make the incorrect assumption that business people are the same throughout the world.

My first encounter with a foreign culture and customs had come in Paris. Allied had been hired to protect three executives, and from a local security agency we retained two Frenchmen: Jean Claude, who spoke English fluently; and Pierre, our driver, who spoke only French. Both men had prior police experience and were highly qualified to work the detail with me.

Pierre drove Jean Claude and me right behind the executives' vehicle to a shopping district near Notre Dame. When the chauffeur parked the executive limo, I instructed Pierre, through Jean Claude's translation, to remain with the two vehicles.

Jean Claude and I moved on foot through the crowded streets, following the executives from shop to shop until they stopped at a quaint café near Notre Dame.

I noticed a beautiful woman with shiny long black hair, dressed in a sequined black micro-mini and black stockings exit her car in front of the restaurant and create a super traffic jam. Drivers craned their necks to catch a look and became entangled in a gridlock.

After about ten minutes of fist-waving motorists honking horns and screaming obscenities, I saw a man standing in the middle of the street trying to direct traffic.

"I don't believe it!" I said. "That's Pierre. He was supposed to stay with the limo! Tell him to return to his post."

Jean Claude weaved through the blocked cars, gave the driver instructions, and came back to the café.

Pierre didn't miss a beat in his whistling, gesturing, traffic-cop routine.

After I sent Jean Claude out to him a second time, the driver reluctantly climbed back into his vehicle, drove a block, and went into a restaurant for a beer and a sandwich.

I was furious. I had Jean Claude tell him to take that sandwich and get back to the limousine, and not to drink. Pierre agreed to return to the parking lot, *after* his beer.

Jean Claude explained in his defense that drivers are allowed to go for food and in France lunch is customarily taken with a couple of beers, or wine, not considered in the law-enforcement community to be alcoholic beverages.

Drinking, abandoning posts, and refusing to follow directions were unacceptable in my profession, in my society, and I fired the driver.

But Paris couldn't hold a candle to the unique customs of Thailand. Thais, in my experience, do not like to confront stressful situations, and often they simply leave rather than deal with them head-on. Also, the basic lifestyle is much slower than America's.

Whatever leads I gave Vallop, follow-up would take much longer than if we investigated them, and matters would get worse if I pushed his operatives to go faster than they were accustomed to working. Because of slow mail delivery, if I didn't call Vallop with information, I could add a couple of months to the investigation.

At midnight I tried to phone him, but the overseas lines were backed up. Finally, about 1 A.M., I got through on a weak, static-plagued connection.

When his secretary answered, I could barely understand her, and I had to repeat Vallop's name several times before she told me in Thai to hold on. I waited a few minutes, and thought the line had gone dead, but just as I began to hang up I heard a man's voice speaking in Thai. My own Thai vocabulary is very limited, so I continued to repeat Vallop's name.

"This is Vallop," the voice suddenly said in English.

"Vallop! Hello! This is Mike Intravia from the United States."

"Mike, how are you, my friend?"

"What is happening on the Shillander investigation?" I asked.

"What investigation? I do not understand."

"The Children of God case," I said.

"Ah, the children you are looking for, yes. I am privileged to work with you."

I slowly gave my Thai associate the leads I had received from Vivian, and hoped he understood. "Please, investigate this information and keep trying to find this family. Do not let anyone know what you are doing. If you find them, please take pictures, and call me immediately."

"I understand what you are asking, Mike. We will start looking for the children."

"I will send you a copy of pictures I have of the children. I will put them on an airplane, which I'd like you to have someone meet. One of the pictures was taken at a refugee camp near Cambodia. If you have agents on the Cambodian border, please have them check. I look forward to seeing you soon, and thank you for your help."

It was late, but I couldn't sleep. My mind wandered through the bustling streets of Bangkok. The last time I had visited the chaotic capital of Thailand, I came close to being robbed.

Scott Biondo and I had tailgated our clients and their wives, who were on a quest for fine pearls, to the outskirts of the city. We saw them safely inside a famous jewelry store that caters to a wealthy clientele. With no place to park, the limo driver had pulled off the narrow street and stopped directly in front of the shop. He sought relief from the scorching heat and waited under a shade tree near the curb.

Scott positioned himself close to the entrance. I stood across the street facing a narrow alleyway running adjacent to the jewelry store.

Looking down the alley, I saw a residential area housing the poor, a drastically deteriorating contrast to the business street. Clothes hung out to dry from each window of those run-down, high-rise tenements. Lean-to shacks made of sheet metal and cardboard boxes lined the alley, dwarfed by the dilapidated apartment buildings. It was truly a sad picture, and a dangerous setting for our operation.

From my vantage point, I watched people milling around on the sidewalks of the busy main street plus those coming and going in the alley, but I couldn't distinguish which ones might wish us ill.

Then two Thais walked out of the alley and stopped, sizing up our vehicles and drivers. Scott moved directly in front of the jewelry store. In the event of a problem, he knew his job was to keep the executive party inside the establishment, whose front door was locked (a general practice in Bangkok), and leave me to handle any difficulties.

The two men turned and continued down the street into the crowd.

Could this be a setup? I wondered.

I saw them return ten minutes later. They glanced at us as they walked by, and disappeared into a crevice shortly after entering the alley.

Scott nodded, signaling that the executives were exiting the store. The coast was clear as they and their wives came out.

Suddenly the two Thais returned.

I moved straight toward them and Scott got between the executives and the alley. One of the Thais stood in a shielding position, blocking Scott's view, as the other lifted his shirt and clasped what appeared to be a blue steel .38 caliber revolver.

Scott and I reached under our jackets for our weapons. Scott's action caught their attention, and the Thai standing shield spotted me at the same time. He said something to his friend, who seemed to freeze with the gun still in his waistband.

The seconds we stood in the face-off played out like minutes in slow motion. The Thais looked at each other and decided it was not a good idea to try to rob these Americans.

The Thai with the weapon released his grip, allowing his shirt to fall back down over his trousers. They turned, moved into the alley, and vanished from sight with the swiftness of a Siegfried and Roy magic act.

Scott had already secured our clients in the back of the limo and told the driver to leave immediately. The vehicle pulled away, carrying four passengers unaware of how close they came to being in the middle of a shootout.

As Scott and I sped off in our security car to catch up with them, I looked down the alley, where crowds of Thais had gathered, but the two who intended to hold us up were long gone into another world.

Now, regardless of physical danger involved in attempting to rescue the Shillander children, I feared any defeat would more likely spring from Thai society itself. I had to be super-sensitive with Vallop, making sure I did nothing to offend him.

And courts in Thailand could present a big problem. For example, business disputes, if allowed to wend through the Thai judicial system, customarily take five to ten years to litigate. To expedite a settlement, two businessmen at loggerheads sometimes take out murder contracts on each other; the survivor wins the suit.

Finally, a Thai judgment for Vivian depended not on right or wrong, but on the amount of influence wielded by the opposing attorneys. The Children of God could and would easily outspend the meager contributions donated by the congregation at First Baptist Church of Sioux Falls.

5

We'll Go for Them

V IVIAN," I SAID INTO THE PHONE a few days after the talk with
Vallop, "this is Mike Intravia. Have you heard anything
from Haugaard about that custody lawsuit?"

"Nothing. I'm getting very anxious."

"Call him. Find out where we stand."

"All right," she said.

"Have you ever sent any registered mail to the children?
Anything we could trace?"

"No. I send letters regular mail. Besides, COG uses post
office boxes."

"Have you mailed gifts for Christmas, or birthdays?"

"No. Just cards. Gifts would be appropriated by the cult."

"How about money orders or checks?"

Bingo.

"Mike! I just remembered, I sent birthday checks to the
children this year. They'd never see cash from me. But I mailed
a check to Caleb just last month."

"Vivian, this is important. Contact your bank and have
them track down those checks. As soon as you get copies, send
them to me."

"I'll get right on it."

"And, Vivian, why not call Brad Beckstrom? See if he can
provide a name for you to contact at the American Embassy in
Thailand. Write that person and try to establish rapport in advance. I'd do it, but the embassy is more likely to respond to the
mother."

Scott Biondo stood in my office door, asking about Vivian,
wondering when he could fly to Thailand.

"Aren't you more interested in your present assignment?" I joked.

Scott headed up a protection detail for Mikhail Baryshnikov, coming to St. Louis the next week to perform at the Fox Theatre.

"Baryshnikov's a piece of cake."

"You look sharp today." He wore a light gray designer suit and classy red tie.

"Yeah. I'm a real fashion plate. Hey, Mike, what about the Shillander case?"

Right. What about it? I thought. Scott's outward impatience mirrored what I felt inside. *But there was nothing we could do.*

"I've got a report for you. It contains all the intelligence and advance information on Baryshnikov."

"Hey, he's in good hands. What about the kids?"

"Okay. I appreciate your enthusiasm. I want you to start playing supervisor. *You* think of what we can fruitfully do that's not being done right now. Maybe you can figure how to pin down the COG location. Vallop's working on it full-time."

"I'll put on my thinking cap."

"Fine. And don't forget Baryshnikov."

"He'll be okay. Trust me. I haven't lost anybody yet."

It was a beautiful October day, and after talking with Scott I drove my cocoa brown Jaguar XJ6—I'm typically a very conservative person, the car being my one luxury—along Lindbergh Boulevard en route to a luncheon appointment with St. Louis detective Sergeant Jim McMillen.

The city blazed in spectacular fall foliage: bright oranges, reds, and golds. Winters here can be cruel, but autumn is unfailingly lovely. The blue sky and crisp air invigorated, and I stepped out of my car in the back parking lot of the Berkeley Police Department with a bounce in my step.

I stuck my head into Chief Bob Stuart's office. We had started together as patrolmen, and I would have been blind not to see his potential. I predicted he would make chief; the only surprise, just a slight one, was how quickly he did it.

"I'm here to apply for a job," I said.

"You're hired," Stuart said. "We could use a nut like you. I hear you'll soon be off to Thailand."

We reminisced for a few moments, then I went to Jim McMullen's office. Mack was short, stocky, muscular, tough, one of the best liked and most competent men on the force. He could be warm and witty, but criminals never saw that side of him.

We had lunch at Garavelli's, cafeteria-style, on Olive Street, and Mack told me things hadn't improved since I left the department. Crime was up. It always seemed to be up.

I was aiming a knife and fork at a roast chicken when my beeper sounded. I went to a pay phone in the corner.

"Sorry to interrupt your lunch," Joyce said, "but Vivian just called. She said to tell you a South Dakota judge has signed the papers, giving her custody of the children. That's good news, isn't it?"

Perhaps more than anyone else in the office, Joyce, herself a mother, agonized long and often about the Shillander children.

"That's *great* news," I said.

Sine qua non news, as a matter of fact, where the investigation was concerned. We couldn't make any moves toward the children without those custody papers.

"Something good happen?" Mack asked, when I returned to the table.

"Yeah."

"But not the ultimate," he judged shrewdly. "If you'd *found* the children, you'd look a lot happier."

Mack was indeed a good detective.

Patti and I discussed the case that evening. "I can't get a fix on when you'll be leaving for Thailand," she said, frowning. On occasions she could be absolutely uncanny about such matters.

"I hope it's not during Thanksgiving or Christmas," I said.

"Something in the middle. Wouldn't bringing the children home be a wonderful Christmas present for Vivian?"

A few days later it seemed possible. I learned the promising information over my car phone as I worked a corporate investigation.

"Scott here. I've got good news, Mike."

"I could use some. What?"

"Vallop called. He has obtained an address for Richard through one of his contacts at Thai Immigration. He used the same address to endorse the check Vivian sent."

"Are you talking post office box?"

"No. Let me give these words a try," he laughed, "and don't you make fun of my pronunciation." He read an address in the Phaya Thai district of Bangkok.

"You need to get Vallop out to that house to eyeball the occupants."

"His investigators have already done that. They talked to people in the area who said Americans fitting the Shillanders' description live there."

"Did Vallop's people see any of the Americans?"

"No."

"I'm on my way to the office. We'll talk."

I hoped finding the children and Richard would really be this easy. *Or* just the children, because COG frequently separates older youngsters from their parents for matters of indoctrination, as in the Richert case when the daughter resided in Mexico and the son in Peru. The answer in such instances is to take the kids you can lay your hands on and tear up the streets tracking down the others.

Everything needed to be in place by the time we located them. The COG routinely moves every couple of months, so when we found the children, the rescue operation had to activate immediately. The actual recovery tactic could not be determined until we got to Thailand, and it could change hour to hour, minute to minute.

Scott had the office buzzing with the news. As I walked inside, I heard him in a rear room, holding everyone captivated with details of the communiqué from Thailand.

"What's going on?" I asked, smiling, knowing every employee of the company had adopted this case.

"This, Mr. Intravia," said Scott, "is an official briefing on AI87–0170."

"You let these people fool around like this?" I said to Don Kissell, who was as caught up in the excitement as everyone else.

"I'm timing them," he said, assuming the role of Scrooge, "so we can dock their pay."

"Time to pack bags?" Scott asked, ever eager, in many respects a younger version of myself.

I hated to throw cold water on everyone's optimism, but, "I have doubts about the Shillanders being in that house," I told them bluntly.

"Vallop's people already talked to neighbors who said the children live there."

"Children *fitting the description* live there."

"Immigration said they live there."

He was right. I just couldn't bring myself to believe we would be this lucky.

"I don't want this information passed on to Vivian," I said.

"She needs a boost," Joyce said.

"I'm sure she does. But what if her children aren't there? What if this is a false alarm?" *And what was the matter with me? Why all the negativism?* But I plunged forward. "The fewer heartbreaks Vivian experiences, the better she'll hold up when it comes time to recover the children."

I hoped they understood the point I made, or at least forgave me for making it. To think one day we may have found them, and then find out the next that we had not would create unbearable disappointment.

"Did Vallop say anything else?" I asked Scott, when we were alone in my office.

"That's about it. He has an active surveillance on the house."

"Did you remind him to take pictures?"

"Yes. Vallop said it might be difficult, unless the kids come onto the street. The house has a wall around it."

"COG houses usually have a wall on the perimeter to conceal members' presence. What about the children? Did he learn anything about them?"

"No. He said record checking is extremely difficult because it's not computerized."

"I want you to contact our travel agent, Teri Schuchman, and have her research all the flights for Bangkok. Then . . ."

"I thought you were Mr. Go Slow."

"Then ask her to print up flight itineraries. Call Vivian, remind her to get Haugaard to obtain certification of those custody documents from the Thai embassy. You need . . ."

"I like this you better than the other one."

"I fear the other one may be right," I said. "Those Thai investigators will have as hard a time positively identifying Americans as you would identifying Thais. There are only two ways we can accept a confirmed sighting: one, if you or I eyeball them, or two, if we get pictures. This case has three phases, Scott. First, locating the children. Second, recovery. And third, getting out of there safely. If we blow any one of those phases, we lose everything. Believe me, my heart says *go*, but my head says *wait*."

After Scott left, I nearly drove myself crazy trying to formulate strategy. The distance made everything a hundredfold more difficult. If the children had been in the next county, the next state, or even the next country, we could just go, and keep going again and again if necessary. But Thailand . . . ten thousand miles. We couldn't shuttle back and forth to Thailand.

Everything was just too speculative. I feared, despite all my preparations, maneuvering, figuring, calculating, we would in the end probably have to act before we saw.

I was working a mid-November surveillance when the bad news came over my car phone.

"Give it to me quickly, Scott," I said.

"I talked with Vallop. Richard and the children have moved."

After all my caveats about not expecting results from that address, still I felt a pang of disappointment when the lead didn't pan out.

"How long ago did they move?"

"Three to six months."

Well, it figured. Undoubtedly the neighbors had seen the Americans some time before. COG members maintain low visibility, and they could just as well have moved as remained hidden behind the wall around the house.

It hit me hard. I wondered whether Scott had thought to ask if Vallop's people had bothered to knock on any doors after discovering the Americans had left the house? I needed to get back to the office and hear the details.

I called ahead to ask Scott not to leave until I talked with him. I was glad we hadn't built up Vivian's hopes, and looking on the bright side, I reasoned that we were only three to six months behind them, not as cold as some trails we'd followed.

As I drove, my mind painted a picture of where they had lived: a two-story house tucked away on a narrow street in Bangkok, invisible to passersby because of the perimeter wall topped with shards of broken glass. Two or three families probably shared the residence, with all children sleeping in one room. The location posed a nightmare for anyone doing surveillance, and an impossible job for an American.

Scott stood in the office lobby with the file in his hand.

"How did Vallop learn they had moved?"

"On a pretense call. He said they couldn't wait any longer without being spotted. The house is on a short street, behind . . ."

"A high wall."

"Right. After a few days they saw some Thai children go in, so they followed them and were told that Richard and the children had moved. I asked Vallop to canvass the areas for leads on where they may have gone, but he says it's not likely anyone will know. Also, he said the picture we sent him had been taken at a refugee camp in the Aranya Prathet area."

"Did you remind him to send someone there to look for a COG settlement?"

"Yes. He said he'd done it."

"Let's find Aranya Prathet," I said, and we walked over to the world map on the wall.

"An interesting little spot," Scott said, pointing it out. "Right here on the border of Cambodia."

"Makes sense. That's where a refugee camp would be located," I said, attempting humor I didn't feel. "Scott, we're on track now, but playing catch-up half-a-world away will be a pain. I'm afraid this case has just begun."

Scott left. I stayed, looking at the map. Thailand, Cambodia, and Laos all came into focus. *They're in one of these places,* I thought, *and we'll go for them.*

COG house in Udon
Thani on immediate
right side of photo.

6

A Sighting

I CALLED VALLOP FOR AN UPDATE AT 1 A.M. our time on November 17, 1987.

"Mike, it is good to hear from you. I have some news. One of the neighbors knew Richard and said he moved to Aranya Prathet near a refugee camp."

I already knew that but didn't want to dwell on problems of communication. "We need to have someone check around Aranya Prathet," I said.

"This has been done, Mike. I have a good man who lives in the area, but you should know it is many hours from Bangkok, on the border of Cambodia, where there is still fighting with the military."

"I understand. And I appreciate any information your investigator can get. Please be sure to tell him *no contact* if he finds Richard or the children. What we would love to have is pictures."

"He has been instructed in this way."

"Scott sends his greetings and says he looks forward to working with you in Thailand."

"Tell Scott I look forward to seeing him also. He is a fine young man. Assure yourself, and him too, that I will do everything I can to find the children quickly."

The pieces of the puzzle seemed to be coming together: a picture showing them at a refugee camp near Aranya Prathet, and now a neighbor who said Richard had taken them back there. Because of the Cambodian civil war, the investigation could become quasi-military if it continued on this course. I

shuddered at the complications of going into an active combat
zone.

Messages were stacked on my desk the next morning, but
one jumped out at me: It came from my number-one client, a
Fortune 500 corporation, involving a trip across Europe on
a three-week protection detail leaving February 3, 1988, for
myself, Scott, and one other agent. I couldn't say no to this
company, but the assignment might coincide with the exact
month we needed to be in Asia.

I dialed South Dakota. During the past several conversations with Vivian, she had become increasingly anxious for
action.

"Remember the picture you sent?" I asked, when I had her
on the line. "We've identified the area of the refugee camp as
Aranya Prathet, which is on the border of Cambodia. We also
found an individual who says Richard has all of the children
with him near Aranya Prathet."

"My God . . . I suppose that's good news. It doesn't surprise me he took them into a place like that. But isn't there still
fighting in that region?"

"Yes. Border skirmishes. Martial law is in effect."

"Does that mean you won't be able to help?" I could hear
her hold her breath.

"No. I believe we'll find them and bring them back to
South Dakota."

"Thank God! I feared if they went into an area like that,
and I suspected they might, you wouldn't go after them. You
know, I planned to call you today. I think I'll go to Bangkok this
week and ask the American Embassy and Thai government to
help me. I'll be there when you're ready to come over, which
hopefully will be in the next couple of weeks."

Oh, brother! Now I held my breath. I was glad we didn't
use picture phones, because my expression conveyed more elo-
quently than any words how I felt about this scheme.

"Vivian, it's not a good idea at this point for you to go to
Thailand."

"Why not?"

"First, pleas to orientals from a nonoriental woman wanting to take children away from their father will fall on
deaf ears. Second, I'm in the dark on how long it will take to

pinpoint their location. Weeks, months, who knows how long? You don't have the resources or the strength to last for months in Thailand. Third, you may be needed here to sign papers or take other legal action, after we do locate the children."

"Yes, but . . ."

"Vivian, I sympathize with your plight, but now is not the time for you to run around willy-nilly. What do you think COG would do if they found you in Thailand, by yourself, trying to take the children from them?"

"I'm not sure. I suppose I would be in danger."

"Don't suppose. Count on it. Please, I need you to hold off and allow us to coordinate everyone's efforts, including yours, into a single recovery operation."

"All right. I'll wait. But it's hard not doing anything."

"I know it is."

"What *can* I do?"

"Make sure your passport is in order. Arrange for someone to take care of Yancha. Ask your travel agent to check flights into Bangkok. If you have a problem, I'll have my agent coordinate for you from St. Louis."

Vivian agreed to every suggestion, which put me on alert. She had become more anxious than I had realized, and I knew it was a matter of time before she flew to Thailand to look for her kids. Each day she became stronger, but her impatience could doom the operation.

A week went by with no word from Vallop. I imagined what the weather would be like in Aranya Prathet: hot, humid, beastly.

Increasing the range of our search to Aranya Prathet escalated the danger level. I would need additional manpower, agents who were more than good investigators. They had to be experienced in working perilous situations, intelligent, brave, resourceful, and, in general, tough customers. Two men jumped to the top of the list; both had international experience—one had worked in foreign countries with me—and each I counted as a friend.

Al Carter, a sergeant with the Ellisville (Missouri) Police Department, is also known to me as Sifu. Al is my chief martial arts instructor, holding the rank of Godan (fifth-degree black belt). He spent four years in the Army in the Security Agency Division, then entered police work. Al lived in the Far East as a child and has made martial arts an integral part of his adult life. In hand-to-hand combat, he is one of the most dangerous men in the world.

Terry Coleman, a sergeant with the Manchester (Missouri) Police Department, had worked with me in Berkeley, and we had survived several dangerous situations in the past. Brave and resourceful, Terry is one of the nation's top experts in firearms and combat shooting. An expert marksman, he was a perfect choice, along with Al Carter, to form the recovery team that Scott and I needed if we were to be successful in Aranya Prathet.

Al and Terry were game, and we spent many hours discussing in-depth basic operational plans. I felt comfortable with them as backup, and they welcomed the challenge.

Joyce handled passports, with Brad Beckstrom lending assistance on visas. Travel agent Teri Schuchman became involved in the case, as she typically does. The travel agent can play a key role in an overseas recovery. In the past Teri often had gone into her office late at night and on weekends to book us on flights out of the country.

Scott had researched Thai law on guardianship and found nothing encouraging. Specifically, I had wondered if Thai courts would enforce Vivian's custody order and compel Richard to release the children once we found them.

The answer was no. Instead, Richard would be summoned to court, thus creating probably insurmountable problems, the most obvious being that he would gather up the children and flee the country. Even if we did get him in front of a judge, Thai courts do not look kindly on divorce, and the laws are stacked heavily in the husband's favor.

Furthermore, the courts are so slow the case likely would take years.

However, Scott had also found "Regulations of the Department of Religious Affairs," which fell under the Ministry of the Interior of the Royal Thai Government. From our interpretation, COG clearly violated several regulations, but whether we could get anyone to listen and help was questionable.

International parental child abduction cases are one of the latest of several serious social disorders that by and large were unknown to the last generation. The U.S. State Department's Office of Citizens Consular Services (CCS) has in the last decade been contacted about some twenty-three hundred cases in which American children had either been abducted by a parent from the United States, or prevented from returning to the United States by a parent.

Recovery, though always difficult, can be made easier if the nation where the children are held adheres to the Hague Convention (twenty-three countries do—Thailand does not), which declares that children wrongfully removed or retained in one of these countries must be returned promptly to the nation where they habitually resided before the abduction or wrongful retention.

The Shillander case was, legally, one of the rarest, most complex, and bewildering of all. In what country, a court would ask, even in a nation abiding by the Hague Convention, did these children "habitually reside"?

The International Society of Private Investigators (ISPI) offers tips on how to proceed in international child retention cases:

• Under the U.S. Department of Health and Human Services, the Office of Child Support Enforcement maintains the Federal Parent Locator Service (FPLS). The primary purpose of this service is to locate parents who are delinquent in child support payments, but the service will also search for parental abductors when requested to do so by a judge or law enforcement agent. Using the abductor's Social Security number, the FPLS searches the records maintained by such federal agencies as the Internal Revenue Service, Veterans Administration, Social Security Administration, Department of Defense, and the National Personnel Records Center. An abductor who has had a connection with any of the above might, even from abroad, renew a connection with one of them.

• To obtain information on requests that may have been made by the abductor to a child's school for the transfer of records, contact the principal of the school. The school will need a certified copy of the custody decree.

• The National Center for Missing and Exploited Children can assist in the preparation of a poster for the missing child. A poster may assist foreign authorities in attempting to locate the child.

• The local prosecutor can be asked to contact the U.S. Postal Inspection Service to see if a "mail cover" can be put on any address in the United States to which the abductor might write.

• Local law enforcement authorities may be asked to obtain, by subpoena or search warrant, credit card records that may show where the abductor is making purchases. In the same manner, efforts may be made to obtain copies of telephone company bills of the abductor's friends or relatives who may have received collect calls from the abductor.

Unfortunately, most of these suggestions constituted such remote long shots that we would have wasted time trying to implement them. Richard wasn't paying U.S. taxes or keeping his Social Security up to date. The children had no American school records to check. Richard had no friends to write in the United States.

The poster idea likely would have been counterproductive. COG members would have spotted the handbills, and Richard would quietly slip into another country with the children in tow.

On November 24, I called Vallop again. It was a Tuesday night, and I had just finished teaching class. Thanksgiving, a special holiday in our family, was only two days away, and the turkey was already thawing for a big dinner at my parents' house.

As usual, the overseas telephone lines were tied up, and I dialed over and over trying to get through. I finally connected and the familiar voice of his secretary answered the phone. She immediately buzzed Vallop.

"Mike, I just received some information about the children. My investigator in Aranya Prathet says they are there, along with Richard."

"That makes me very happy, my friend. Has your agent taken any pictures?"

"No. Not yet. He saw them walking in Aranya Prathet and followed them home. He is watching the house."

"Your investigator has done a good job. Please have him

take pictures right away, and you can fax them to me. Also, the Cambodian border region is very dangerous, as you know, so I plan to bring two more agents with Scott and me. Can you provide several off-duty policemen and the necessary weapons?"

"You are very correct. Around Aranya Prathet, one must be prepared at all times. You can be ambushed driving down the road. I can provide the people and equipment we need."

"We'll make preparations for the trip, but won't leave until you send the pictures. We must be sure your man has found the right family."

"I understand. We will send pictures as soon as my investigator can obtain them."

I couldn't sleep that night. A thousand thoughts rushed through my mind, and adrenaline flowed through my body.

I believed locating the Shillander children would be relatively easy, but recovering them extremely difficult.

I wondered if the Thai investigator could have made a mistake. Mobilizing the operation was a major decision, particularly considering the expenses involved in flying halfway around the world.

I told myself that Aranya Prathet is a small village with probably a minimum of white faces. Surely the Thai investigator had been able to correctly identify Richard and the children from the pictures I had sent Vallop. However, I kept reflecting on how difficult it would be for me to identify Thais in the United States from an old photo—the old they-all-look-alike mistake. I had to stay committed to my original plan of positive identification.

I tossed and turned in a half sleep until 3:30 A.M., then crawled out of bed. Patti woke up and asked what was wrong. I told her I just couldn't sleep and wanted to go downstairs to my study for awhile. Since our talk on the first day of the case, I really hadn't discussed it much with her, and I especially had avoided mentioning the Aranya Prathet development. There was no need to tell her I was leaving until it was actually time to go. And when that happened, she would see me off to Bangkok, not to a demilitarized zone setting like a powder keg on the Cambodian border.

After dawn finally put an end to the restless night, I left the house before Patti, Erica, or Tanya woke up. I called Scott from my car and told him I believed the children had been found. "We need to shift our caseloads to other agents," I said.

"Then we're going?"

"I think so. We may take others."

"All right!"

"Clear your calendar. Once we get there, no telling when we'll come back."

I called Vivian and told her we might leave soon. She cried for joy and tried to pry details about the children from me, details I did not know.

Thanksgiving that year was different from any I had known. We went to my parents' home, about an hour out of St. Louis in a quaint rural community called Elsberry, where they had retired.

My dad, a decorated gunnery sergeant during World War II, had grown up on "The Hill," the Italian section of St. Louis that produced baseball players Joe Garagiola and Yogi Berra. Serfino (I never called him that, of course) worked hard all his life, selling produce, providing for his six kids, and treasuring my mom, Louise, who was born and raised on an isolated Missouri farm. Together they gave us a loving, stable environment that emphasized family and family values.

The fire crackled that day in the fireplace near a table completely covered with turkey and other usual delights of the holiday feast. My whole family was there: my two brothers, John and Joe, and three sisters, Pat, MaryAnn, and Carol, plus their spouses and children.

I was the one who *wasn't* there, at least not completely. My thoughts kept jumping ahead to a trek through the Thai jungle, and I couldn't concentrate on anything else. I had told Patti I might be leaving for Bangkok in the next few days, and she had hit me with a barrage of questions. I answered by telling her we had found a house where the Shillanders might be living. True enough. I just left out the Aranya Prathet part. I also didn't tell her about Terry Coleman and Al Carter. Patti had been married to me long enough to know that when I took that pair along, I anticipated trouble in big doses.

Sitting on the hearth, watching one imaginary jungle skirmish burn against another in the fireplace, a tug on my sleeve brought me back to Elsberry and my nine-year-old nephew, Chad Menard. Chad lives in Atlanta with my sister Carol and her husband Rene. They moved from St. Louis after Rene took an executive position with a major corporation.

Chad seemed to be falling into his uncle's footsteps. He already had studied martial arts and aspired to work for Allied Intelligence full-time after college. When visiting St. Louis he helped out in our office and had done some research for me in Atlanta, clipping articles about cults from the Atlanta newspapers, particularly articles about the Children of God.

"Uncle Mike, is there something wrong?"

"What makes you ask?"

"You've been sitting by yourself a lot today and look kinda lost."

"Sorry if I seem rude; I'm just preoccupied with something. Want to hear about it?"

"Sure."

"I have to go overseas to Thailand and rescue some children for their mother."

"Can I go?"

"I'm afraid this one's not for you, Bud."

"Where is the children's father, Uncle Mike?"

"In Thailand, we think. He has the children with him and hasn't let their mom see them for more than three years. They're in one of those cult groups that you and I have talked about before."

"Don't worry. If anybody can bring the kids back, it's you," he said with a reassuring smile. "How about a turkey sandwich? I'll fix it for you."

"Sure. With a lot of mayonnaise."

▲
Area near where
the children were
recovered.

7

Half a World Away

FRIDAY I HOPED THE PHONE WOULD RING with news from Thailand. But Friday passed. So did Saturday and Sunday. I got calls from Scott, Vivian, Terry Coleman, Al Carter, and Teri at the travel agency. All of us itched for action.

Sunday night, unable to wait any longer, I called Vallop. I had become frustrated not knowing and holding everybody on standby. The worst, though, was not knowing, especially for Vivian—humans can adjust to almost anything if they just comprehend clearly what it is and thus can reconcile themselves to reality. I felt like a race horse that had been left standing in the starting gate too long. It was Monday in Thailand and they were well into their workday when I finally got through to Vallop.

"I know why you are calling," Vallop said. "I was about to call you. My investigator went to the house under pretense and knocked on the door. A man answered with two of the children standing behind him. He spoke in broken English, and obviously was not an American. Possibly European. At close range my investigator could see they were not the Shillander children. We have not located them."

My heart sank and I knew Vivian would take a deeper plunge to the depths. I cursed myself for having raised her hopes and dreaded giving her the news.

I told Vallop to have his investigator continue checking the area and to visit some of the nearby towns.

Vallop is a professional. I knew he regretted that one of his agents had spoken too soon and too optimistically. The investigator had probably spotted the only white children in the village, followed them to a house, and because of the coincidence assumed he had the right family.

It was time to move on, but I nonetheless put off until late the next morning the task of bearing ill tidings.

As expected, the news nearly broke Vivian's heart. She had allowed herself to believe that the ordeal was nearly over when in fact it was just beginning. She had fantasized about holding April, John, Caleb, and Tito safely in her arms in a matter of days.

My sympathy again went out to this mother who ached to be reunited with her brood. Even though the setback shook her, I believed she still retained sufficient strength to continue. I had to shelter her more from the stressful roller-coaster rides of the investigation. Like the Thai investigator, I'd behaved too optimistically.

A week later Vivian was determined to leave for Thailand. I received calls from Brad Beckstrom and Steve Haugaard. They had been trying to dissuade Vivian, worrying for her safety and believing that the timing was wrong. They were right on both counts. They had managed to persuade her to wait—but they weren't sure for how long.

Vallop called during the week with new information. His investigator still had not found any sign of Richard or the children in Aranya Prathet, but had checked a refugee camp and "verified" through a neighbor that they *had been* there. The people he contacted at the camp were uncooperative and refused to tell him anything else. The investigator had begun his check of nearby towns.

Was it possible the Thai neighbor had lied? Or had Richard fed him a fabricated story to throw searchers off track? Could people at the refugee camp be hiding Richard and the children?

Perhaps the investigator simply didn't know what he was doing. If so, he had plenty of company among private detectives I've known in the United States. Regardless, if we didn't find the Shillanders in the next week, I suspected all our efforts to date would have been for naught, and we'd be starting over from square one.

Possibly the Shillanders had packed and moved. It would happen anyway, sooner or later; they had been in Thailand a long time. I asked Vallop if he had a contact in Immigration who could find out if Richard and the children had left the country. He said yes, but it would take time to get the information, and its reliability would be questionable because documents frequently disappear. Also, if Richard and the children had departed through a small border checkpoint, there might be no record at all.

A week into December Vivian's impatience got the best of her. She called to tell me she was leaving and had already purchased her ticket. I knew it was useless to debate the decision, despite its utter wrongness. I did understand, though, why she felt driven to go.

This development opened another can of worms to further complicate the job. I worried that COG would learn of her presence and order Richard to pull up stakes. Also, COG might kidnap her, leaving us with *five* people to bring back.

Investigators need to control their contacts as well as their clients, and I feared I wasn't controlling either.

Vivian had asked Scott and me to come with her. I wanted to be on the scene, directing operations, rather than chafing half a world away, but it just wasn't the right move to make. Funds were minimal, and the leads weren't hot enough to justify our going yet. We could end up staying for months and discover that they had long ago vamoosed. Working from St. Louis might be slower, but at this point it was logical and economical.

Sitting tight hardly qualified as a heroic pose, and perhaps those who didn't know me well thought I didn't care deeply enough. The truth was that, except for Vivian, no one craved action over inertia more than I did. But action, in this instance, would be mere grandstanding.

Vivian caught a Northwest Airlines flight, which took her to San Francisco and on to Bangkok. She had arranged to stay at the Baptist Guest House, run by Americans.

Vivian was edgy, nervous, and frightened, but determined to push her cause along. I dearly hoped leads would develop and we would soon join her in Thailand.

She called as soon as she arrived in the Far East and said she had already mailed me copies of the birthday checks she had sent the children.

Thus, the next piece of evidence arrived in the form of photocopies of the bank drafts issued by First Sioux Falls

National Bank. Three checks had been sent during 1987: the first to Tito (Francisco) on February 4, the second to April on March 20, and the third to Caleb on August 11.

Tito's had been cashed in March 1987 at the Thai Farmers Bank in Pratunam Patoomwan. April's was cashed on April 27 at the Banque Indosuez. Caleb had cashed his check, with his father, on September 29 at the Bank of Ayudhya, Ltd., in Bangkok.

The news was reassuring. If they were still in Bangkok cashing a check at the end of September, I thought it likely they were still there. The most difficult lead to develop in an international case is locating the country where the tracking will begin, but since we had narrowed the world down to a single nation, our chances of success increased a thousand percent.

I called Vallop and asked him to check the Thai banks for an account in the name of Richard Shillander. I doubted Richard maintained one—most COG members keep no money (it's all funneled to Berg and other leaders), much less a bank account—but I would have been remiss in not checking. And for all we knew, Richard himself could have by now advanced to the position of leader. Besides, criminals make mistakes, and I viewed COG as a professional criminal. The cult members are masters at hiding in little corners of Third World countries, covering their tracks, and using phony names as they prey on the poorest of the poor.

I stayed in close touch with Brad Beckstrom and Steve Haugaard. We worked as a team to avoid the shotgun effect of scattering and weakening our efforts.

Family, business, and personal life got put on hold. Each day I hoped to receive news that would put me on a plane to Thailand. Teri Schuchman called in daily status reports of flight schedules, so we could literally time our departure and arrival down to the minute.

Friends invited Patti and me out to dinner, or Patti would ask me to go somewhere with her. Tanya and Erica wanted to know if I would be home for Christmas. I couldn't satisfy any of them. Our lives hung in limbo more than ever after Vivian left for Thailand.

She called from Bangkok, bubbling with renewed hope. She had met Ed Wehrli of the American Embassy, and said he seemed eager to help.

I masked my doubts, knowing American officials are extremely limited in foreign countries. Sure they would meet, discuss, and direct her to offices that might be able to assist, but everything would be done strictly by the book. Embassies are extremely cautious about getting involved with American citizens who enter a foreign country to recover children and take them out.

Vivian wanted to meet my contacts in Thailand, a request I absolutely opposed. The contact should always answer directly to the investigator supervising the case, and have no relationship with the client. Managing investigators abroad is touchy and difficult, with customs and attitudes to be carefully maintained. Clients who become demanding or emotional weaken the supervisor-operative link, and the investigation suffers.

Another major difficulty is the ego conflict some investigators experience when under the direction of another detective. All these ingredients can create a corrosive mix that may destroy any chances of success. The likelihood is so imminent that sometimes I back out of a case rather than put my client in contact with foreign associates.

"Vivian," I tried to explain, "I'm afraid you might try to direct the Thai investigators yourself and become directly involved in the case. Believe me, that situation almost always spells disaster."

"I wouldn't," she vowed.

"Maybe not intentionally, but your desperation to find the children would gnaw at you and finally make the temptation irresistible."

She didn't seem happy.

"Vivian, trust me. Remember, my decisions are always designed in your best interest, and the children's."

Vallop called a day later with an update offering no hope. His investigators had combed the little towns near Aranya Prathet and were unsuccessful in finding Richard, the children, or any sign of a COG settlement. The contact in Thai Immigration also gave no cause for optimism.

Vallop's investigators worked slowly, but they did their job. Slow was the usual pace for all business in Thailand, but that was not necessarily a negative. There is probably no place in the world where people work at the fast pace of Americans, and that fast pace is not always ideal, either. Understanding this cultural difference was imperative to keeping the investigation alive and obtaining optimum results.

Late at night I sat in my dark office, hating the inactivity, wishing I could be up and at it, breaking into a COG house, putting a real fear of God into Richard, something . . . anything.

Multicolored lights twinkled on the Christmas tree in the darkened reception area, and the radio played "Silent Night." I tried to imagine not seeing Tanya and Erica at Christmas, or any other time for three years. If I had to trade places with Vivian, God only knew what I would do to find them. Vivian did not help by being in Thailand, but I could empathize. I couldn't decide who was the most victimized, the children or her. I had to find them and bring them home. It would eat at me for years if I didn't.

I have had two cases that will always sadden me, and they surface to haunt me every year during Christmas, my time to remember. Both were young girls who were kidnapped and disappeared without a trace. The parents of each were really fine people and I grew close to them, but I never found their daughters. I didn't think I could take adding April, John, Caleb, and Tito Shillander to that memory. I know it's impossible to go through life without disappointments, yet logic doesn't make me feel any better.

I sat in momentary peace, with "White Christmas" on the radio and outside my window. I wanted to be off for Thailand, but all the leads were coming up empty. I had been pushing Vallop and needed to be careful. I couldn't be sure how he or his investigators would respond if the case became more intense.

We had been focusing the search primarily on Richard, and I wondered if we should concentrate more on the children. A lead could be hidden somewhere in their paper trail. I decided to ask Vallop to look into the entrance of two of them into Thailand. I worried that I would burn up his contact with the burden of checking on all four.

On cold, snowy December 20, 1987, the day before winter officially began, Patti and I took Tanya and Erica out to dinner and to browse the malls. Bright decorations and lovely Christmas carols reminded us how lucky we were to be together.

And so did my beeper when it went off on our way home: a message from Vivian.

I called her back from my study. She was not in her room, so the front desk clerk at the Baptist Guest House put me on hold and located her for me.

"How are things over there?" I asked.

"I thought they were going good, Mike. Everyone seemed to be cooperating, but it's turned out to be just a big bunch of talk. They're willing to gab with me, but no one puts actions to their words."

"Vivian, the embassy's hands are tied when it comes to domestic matters. They'll give advice, but there isn't a lot more they can do."

"Well, I'm here now and I can't give up. I've come too far. Have you heard anything lately?"

"Nothing."

"Mike, I need the names and telephone numbers of your contacts. I want to talk to them."

"We discussed this last time, Vivian, and it's still not a good idea. It will accomplish nothing."

"Mike, they actually are employed by me. I'm running out of things to do over here and need to start working with them." Her voice conveyed aggravation, frustration, and anger.

"My policy . . ."

"Forget your policy! I need my children. They need me. I want the names of those contacts so I can be sure they're working."

"Vivian, why did you hire me?"

"I suppose because you know what you're doing."

"Was there another reason?"

"I trusted you."

"If you lose that trust and begin second-guessing, you'll jeopardize our only chance of finding the children. I know you want to help, but you'll only hurt your cause. Now, I'm not going to put you and my contacts together."

The phone went quiet for a moment. Vivian had either lapsed into shock or awakened to reality. I sympathized with her plight, but she did not think clearly, and her passion to find the children could destroy our efforts, probably by alarming COG.

"Will I ever get to meet those contacts?"

"Yes. As soon as I come to Bangkok. But even then, I'll still be directing them."

"I'm scared, Mike. Nothing seems to be going right. I'm afraid we won't find the children. When I came here I was filled with hope, but now I just don't know."

"I understand, Vivian. But I need your trust and patience. Otherwise, we really can't succeed."

"I do trust you. It's just hard. Will you be here soon?"

"I think so."

"Tell Brad and Steve I talked to you."

"I will."

"I hope to see you soon, Mike." Vivian had trapped herself in Thailand. It had to be difficult knowing she had traveled ten thousand miles, could possibly be as close as a few blocks from her children, yet as far away as if she had remained in Sioux Falls.

I called Steve and Brad and told them I was worried about Vivian handling the stress and disappointment of her trip. They expressed the same feelings, and said the entire First Baptist congregation prayed for her every day.

8

Good News on the Heels of Bad

ONCE AGAIN HOPE FLARED when two days before Christmas I received a call from Vallop. He had developed a new lead: An American man accompanied by four children had been seen passing out literature in Khon Kaen, a town midway between Laos and Cambodia. According to Vallop's investigator, one of the children was a young girl fitting April Shillander's description.

Vallop had dispatched several more agents to Khon Kaen to track down the family, and I prepared to leave St. Louis. If it turned out to be Richard and the children, the danger existed that they would move before we got there. Should the Thai investigators identify the children, they were instructed to conduct a twenty-four-hour surveillance until we arrived.

We waited minute by minute. The travel agent purchased tickets for Scott and me. Terry Coleman and Al Carter were placed on standby.

Christmas Eve dawned hectic, with last-minute shopping on the agenda. I really didn't expect to leave on Christmas Day, though I would have to if the sightings were confirmed. But I figured it would take at least two days to track down the children, photograph them, and fax the pictures for verification.

I didn't tell Patti what went on, but surely she knew, what with frantic phone calls, my impatience on Christmas Eve, and the travel bag I had packed and stuck in the rear of our closet.

Still, that evening with Patti and the girls was marvelous. Erica, eight, was excited—perhaps for the last time—over Santa's visit and had baked cookies to energize his toy delivery. We had the fireplaces glowing with warm fires and Christmas music filled the house.

Erica worried about Santa. "Dad, we have fires in both fireplaces. He might not stop by our house."

"Of course he will, Honey."

"But he might be afraid of getting burned."

"Okay. I'll put out the fire in the living room so Santa can come down the chimney right next to the Christmas tree."

Christmas Day began with church. I grew up attending St. Kevin's Catholic Grade School, where we celebrated with processions and beautiful songs proclaiming the birth of Jesus. Christmas Mass is an event my family looks forward to as much as the gifts under the tree in the morning.

We spent the rest of the day with Patti's family and mine. Her parents, like my own, had raised six children. And her father, William Bazzle, like mine, was also a World War II hero. He had been rescued after his ship sank in the Pacific.

Inevitably the Shillander case became a topic of conversation, and we sadly wondered what Vivian's Christmas must be like. She had spent it without her children, alone in a distant country, with uncertainty and fear as companions. Patti said, "Who knows what's happening over there? Maybe God chose this day to start delivering her children from the cult."

A nice thought, but no such miracle occurred.

Vallop called on December 28. His investigators had located a COG settlement—several families living in a house—in Khon Kaen, and he had established a surveillance to spot Richard or the children. But several days had passed without a sighting.

One of Vallop's men had then hoisted himself up a wall, elbows perched on top, legs dangling, to look through the barbed-wire fencing that prevented further progress. He saw a small older-model car with the trunk open and suitcases setting directly behind it on the driveway. He observed a male subject walk out the front door and place another bag in the trunk.

Suddenly a large dog attacked the investigator, barking and snapping at his dangling legs. The Thai quickly dropped onto the street and escaped the dog. He told his partner what he had seen and left the area for a short time to tend his dog bite (Thailand leads the world in per capita rabies cases).

The surveillance team pulled round-the-clock duty, remained in place as Vallop and I talked, and the suitcase-filled vehicle had not left the compound. The man packing the car appeared to be an American, but not Richard. The investigators had questioned some of the neighbors and were told about a cult passing out religious literature. The name of the group: the Children of God.

I believed we were close and might even have found them. Vallop felt the same, and wanted to know if I would now be coming to Bangkok. He would arrange for us to have immediate transportation to Khon Kaen. He said we'd face possible ambushes on the road and that we needed to be prepared, which called for Terry Coleman and Al Carter to be in on the recovery.

I told Vallop to continue the surveillance until he identified the residents of the COG house. I also repeated my request that he check with Immigration on two of the children, April and John.

I had to wonder if maybe I did operate too cautiously. Even Vallop was hinting that I should come to Thailand. My heart screamed *yes*, but my head whispered *no*. With difficulty, I heeded the softer voice for a few more days.

It appeared the group might be changing locations, and a COG settlement typically doesn't move from one side of a city to another. If the cult members were leaving, they would probably go to a different part of Thailand, or to another country altogether. I imagined it would be extremely difficult to relocate them once they left.

Teri Schuchman booked us on Northwest Airlines to Bangkok for December 31, the only available flight. This time of the year is very popular in the Far East, where it's the height of the summer tourist season.

I might be celebrating New Year's Eve over the Pacific. I dearly hoped so.

But another problem slowly edged itself into the picture: my commitment to protect our biggest client on a three-week trip to Europe beginning February 3. The company depended on my being there, and a substitute would be unacceptable.

On the morning of New Year's Eve, I had not received any word from Thailand. I had to make a decision about that Northwest Airlines flight; it was almost impossible without an update from Vallop. It was late in Thailand, but I managed to reach him.

"The house is a COG settlement," he said. "We know this, but we have not seen the people you are looking for."

"Are your men on surveillance?"

"No. They must be off. It is the holiday."

I bit my tongue. "Please have them resume as soon as possible."

"Yes. I will do that. Also, I checked Immigration, as you asked. It seems visas for the Shillander children must be renewed by January 28, 1988."

Good news on the heels of the bad! I wanted to give Vallop a hug.

"That means," I said, "we'll be able to find out the new address when they report."

"Yes. It may take a few days, or longer, depending on which office they report to, but we can find this out."

"Thank you, my friend. We should be seeing you very soon."

I arrived at work bright and early on the first day of 1988, knowing what my next move had to be. I trusted Vallop, but not his people. For all I knew, they may have been stopping by the house from time to time and considered that a continuous surveillance.

I had called Scott and asked him to meet me at work on this first holiday of the new year. I also called Terry and Al, advising that it didn't appear they would be going to Thailand.

Scott walked into my office.

"When are we leaving?" he asked.

"*We* aren't going. *You* are."

"I don't understand."

"Get a cup of coffee. Bring a legal pad. We have a lot to discuss."

I had to cover every base before sending Scott to Bangkok. I knew it was time. What with Vivian close to falling apart and my certainty that Richard and the children were in Thailand, I needed to have better supervision over the Thai investigators.

I had been dealt a trump ace: *The visas had to be renewed by January 28, 1988.* We were closing in on Richard.

"When do I leave?" Scott asked.

"Tomorrow at 8:50 A.M., arriving in Bangkok on the third at 10:55 P.M., on Northwest Airlines Flight 27. I talked with Vallop last night, Scott. He had no news on the surveillance in Khon Kaen. In fact, his agents took New Year's Eve and New Year's off—typical problem of working in foreign countries and part of the reason I need to send you. We're close, but not close enough for both of us to go. Listen up: Vallop said the children's visas expire on January 28."

"That will tell us if they're still in the country."

"Right. But they may choose to leave in the next few weeks rather than renew the visas. Vallop has good contacts in Immigration, and, depending on how far they'll go to help, there may be a chance to find the Shillanders, or at least gain enough ground to get one step behind them. I'm afraid that without one of us there, this could slip through our hands. Frankly, I'm as worried about Vivian as I am about the Thais."

"I feel bad for her."

"Me, too, but I'm sure things have gotten worse instead of better since the last time she called. You need to keep one eye on her and one on the investigation. She's very emotional and I'm afraid she'll start knocking on doors looking for her children and get herself into deep trouble."

"Finding trouble isn't hard in Bangkok."

"You have a tough job. You need, tactfully, to persuade the Thais to pick up the pace. Once you make a positive identification, I'll join you and we'll coordinate the recovery."

"What if I get a crack at recovering the children before you make it to Thailand?"

"I trust your judgment. You make the call. Remember, Vivian has to be present to take custody. Be very careful. The recovery phase is the most dangerous and legally sensitive part of the whole operation. I'd like to be there to coordinate it. A million things can go wrong."

"I won't hesitate if there's an opportunity to do it safely."

We spent several hours discussing the case and the sensitive issues of managing both the Thai investigators and an emotional, desperate client. I knew Scott was a good decision maker and would think hard before acting. I had decided to direct the investigation through him, but if we lost contact, I had faith he would do the right thing.

That evening I called Vivian and told her Scott would be on his way the next morning. "That's the first good news I've had in weeks," she said.

As I suspected, the red tape had gotten thicker, wound tighter, and she had become even more confused and heartbroken. The news of Scott's imminent arrival sparked new hope, and when our conversation ended she sounded upbeat and optimistic: the roller-coaster syndrome. I agreed that Scott could introduce her to Vallop, but insisted Scott alone would coordinate the Thais through me.

Vivian met Scott at Don Maung Airport—remarkably, the first face-to-face contact any of us had with her. Everything had been by phone and letter.

Vivian greeted Scott warmly. She had come to the airport in a small bus with a local missionary group who had driven there to pick up a volunteer.

It was a long ride into Bangkok for Scott, who already had traveled for many hours. The missionaries sang songs en route as they drove the alley-size streets he had not seen for almost a year.

Vivian impressed Scott—and me, later—as a good, decent, sincere person trying to put her tangled life together. She had short black hair, stood five feet, three inches tall with a medium build. She wore a simple, attractive dress, her dark eyes sad and haunting even though a smile played on her face.

The bus dropped Scott and Vivian off at the guest house, where they talked until 1:30 A.M. Scott, weary from the long flight, told her he needed to get some rest. He walked into the quiet streets of Bangkok, found a taxi, and made his way to the Ambassador Hotel.

Scott and Vivian met that afternoon, and he gave her an in-depth briefing on our plans. The day slipped by quickly. Scott called Vallop and made an appointment for the next day.

They met the morning of January 5 in the lobby of the Ambassador, which is similar to our own Holiday Inns. Vallop had one of his investigators with him.

Recognized as perhaps the top private investigator in Thailand, the forty-eight-year-old Vallop projected the distinguished appearance of a successful professional. Big for a Thai man—five feet, nine inches tall and 160 pounds—he had in earlier years been a boxing champion, a title more prestigious in Thailand than it is in the United States. Still in excellent shape, the former champ teaches Thai boxing in Bangkok.

Scott viewed the two men he talked with as a study in contrasts. The always dapper Vallop, impeccably dressed in a tailor-made silk suit accentuating his firm physique, moved with an air of confidence and command. Kasame, his investigator, looked more like the ever-rumpled Lieutenant Columbo of television fame, shoulders slouched under his modest working attire.

Kasame, a few years older than Vallop, had worked the streets as a law-enforcement official and lacked his boss's savoir-faire. He spoke fair English and tried to impress his American counterpart with boasts of his seniority and sharp detecting skills. This Thai's plain round face was full of friendliness and he showed an eagerness to help. But Scott recognized that he would require close supervision.

During the coming days Scott worked closely with Kasame. They had the number of a COG post office box and attempted to learn when the cult picked up its mail, but post office officials had no way of knowing for sure. We didn't put surveillance on the box; it might take a week or more for someone to show, and the odds weighed heavily against that individual being connected with Richard's group.

Scott met with local prosecutors to determine the Thai laws that would affect our recovery of the children. Everywhere he got the same story: To recover the children from the father, Vivian must go to court.

That could cost thousands of dollars, might last for years, and the mother would likely lose.

Scott called every night, giving me the day's news, and we discussed possible avenues he could pursue. Early on he became totally disheartened at the prospect of going to court if Richard didn't simply give up the children. There had to be, he said, another way.

Sometimes, but not often, there just isn't an answer, but the majority of time, condone it or not, a loophole exists. We had to find one.

It seems most legal minds know what you *can't* do, but they fail to take the time to locate the loophole that stays within the boundaries of the law and provides a chance. I urged Scott to get a second, third, or fourth legal opinion, if necessary.

I thought about Vivian's children constantly and the only lifestyle they had ever known, being dragged from house to house, village to village, country to country, always living with other families, hiding from those who would love them, ever prepared to pull up stakes and leave in a heartbeat. April had never had her own room, a stereo, a phone to while away endless hours gabbing with friends—trappings many young American girls take for granted. And the Shillander boys never enjoyed a treehouse in the backyard, going through school with the same group of chums, Little League baseball, or a family dog to romp with and love. None of them had ever painted on ghoulish faces for Halloween trick-or-treat or gotten a bellyache from eating too much chocolate at Easter.

Instead of skipping through the carefree days of childhood, they grew up on the twisted teachings of Moses Berg who was full of suggestions on how to bilk money from strangers.

Some of Berg's teachings endorsed sex for the young: "I practice what I preach, and I preach sex, boys and girls. Hallelujah! God created boys and girls to have children by about the age of twelve."

Berg's daughter Deborah had explained the derivation of the phrase *Flirty Fishing*: "Dad got the terminology from fishing, what Jesus said in the Bible, to go out and fish for men. And so he was going to use the women to fish for the men to bring them into the kingdom of God through flirting. Only the flirting was more than flirting, it was actually, you know, religious prostitution."

On January 10, 1988, Scott called and gave me a rundown of his first week's work.

"Mike, I'm sorry, but it's mostly negative," he said. "I met with a Captain Seehanat, a lawyer here, and he agrees with every other attorney I've consulted. The only means of recovering the children is for Vivian to take Richard to court."

"We can forget that."

"Well, there's no legal method to rescue the children. Seehanat says any alternative will be considered kidnapping, and we'll wind up in a Thai slammer."

"I don't buy that line. There has to be another way. We've faced this problem before in other countries, including America, and they're always quick to say, 'Don't do it; it's kidnapping.' Have you asked about legal loopholes?"

"Any idea I come up with, they shoot down by citing law."

"So what do *you* think we should do?"

"I don't have a solution—not a legal one."

Grabbing John, April, Caleb, and Tito and making a run for it was illegal. As an ex-cop I couldn't travel that route. Too much of my life had been spent enforcing laws, not breaking them. "We have to take their law," I said, "and keep looking for an answer that works for them, and works for us, too. I think we'll find it." I *hoped* we'd find it. "What about other leads?"

"Not good. I talked to a military contact, Lieutenant Colonel Twan, who did some checking at the refugee camps. According to him, the Shillanders haven't been at any of the camps in the past several months. I also met with the Cultural and Religious Affairs Department, which claimed the COG is operating in the country illegally. I don't believe they'll do anything, though."

"How about Immigration?"

"Talked to them yesterday. They believe Richard is still in the country. He left and returned in September 1985—a trip to Bangladesh. In March 1987, he went to the Philippines, returning on April 4, 1987."

"That's about the time Philippine authorities made a big bust in Manila. They arrested COG members on charges of prostitution and deported them. It's probably why Richard went to the Philippines. Evidently he's rising in his world and might be working into a leadership position," I suggested.

"I also have another problem," Scott said, "and it could get serious. I think Vivian, bless her heart, is losing it. She calls me at all hours of the night to talk about the case. She's cooked up a wild plan to go out and hang around the hotels, where COG members may be witnessing, to look for leads."

"This is a terrible time for her. She's worn down and over-reacting—wanting to go into hotels proves that," I said. "Vivian has too much time on her hands; so put her to work. Send her to a government office to talk with someone. You know how long that can take. At least it will keep her busy and give her a sense of helping. And make decisions *for* her. The responsibility for the case is ours, and she depends on us to lead."

Scott tried, but he couldn't control Vivian. She was a time bomb waiting to explode and Kasame set the bomb ticking. "Why," he asked her, "if we locate the children, is it necessary to wait for the *boss* from the United States to arrive?"

"Yes, why is that?" Vivian asked Scott. He explained again that we would have only one chance, anything and everything could go wrong, and it would be best to have me there because of my experience.

Scott had the authority, if the opportunity arose, to make a recovery, but I didn't want the decision in Vivian's or Kasame's hands.

Scott reiterated to Vivian and Kasame the problems we could encounter getting the children out of the country, and assured them I had an airline ticket and could leave in a matter of hours. Their mouths said, "We understand," but Scott read another response in their faces.

9

We Have Found Them!

I NEEDED ADVICE AND KNEW just the person to see. Robert Burke has had the greatest influence on every aspect of my career, but especially in the areas of executive protection and international operations. For the Shillander case I sought him out once again, meeting him for lunch at the Breckenridge Frontenac Hotel in its elegant restaurant, Provinces.

Bob Burke is a retired assistant director of the U.S. Secret Service and is recognized as one of the top professionals in the world in foreign intelligence and the protection of dignitaries. He has had a most colorful career, heading up security for presidents, prime ministers, and royalty; and he has given me literally hundreds of hours of his time. He is a mentor and a good friend, as well as an expert on the Far East. I wanted to hear any suggestions he might have regarding Vivian's case.

"I have a case," I said, getting to the point of our meeting, "that involves children in the COG. I think it's going to take me to Thailand."

"Isn't that the cult you recovered the children from in Mexico and Peru?"

"The same one, only this time there are four children who haven't seen their mother in more than three years."

Burke folded his hands in his lap, leaned back, seemed to stare at the ceiling. "Thailand," he said. "I spent a lot of time in that part of the world during the Vietnam era, and have been back since. It has changed a lot, but no matter the change, you have your work cut out for you. Is the mother going to be able to hold up for you?"

"I'm not sure. She's still recovering from her own battle with COG."

"One wonders how people get trapped in such a position."

"My problem, Bob, is Thailand and Thai law. This has to be done legally. That means . . ."

"Going through the court system."

"Right. And women aren't exactly treated equally there."

"I would say you don't stand a chance in a Thai court."

"That leaves kidnapping and a very good chance of ending up in an Asian jail."

"What if you could recover them without kidnapping?"

"I don't see how. The husband is not going to turn them over to us."

"He might."

"How?"

"Mike, think about it. He won't give them back, not knowingly, and you can't snatch them. Think on it, my friend, I have faith in you."

"What's happening?" I said to Jackie Corey, who called me later that afternoon.

"Vivian's expenses, as you can imagine, have far outdistanced her money coming in, even with the help she's receiving from Sioux Falls. I may have a solution, at least a partial one."

"What is it?" I knew Jackie Corey was resourceful and relentless whenever a child turned up missing—doubly so when it involved COG—but nothing could have prepared me for this latest idea.

"I ran an idea up the flagpole and someone saluted it. The producers of Geraldo Rivera's show have expressed interest in Vivian's case. The exposure wouldn't hurt. It could put pressure on the Thai authorities."

"I don't know that they watch Geraldo," I said, joking, though indeed they would learn about any coverage featuring their country.

"I don't think the idea is that far out, Mike."

"What would they intend to do?"

"Film the recovery. The show wouldn't air until well after you got the children back. Geraldo would probably go with you."

This brainstorm, after peeling away layers of negatives, I thought, *might* produce a positive or two. I didn't like the idea of tripping over Geraldo, and we might come up as empty as he did in Al Capone's vault, but the chances of running into problems with authorities in Thailand would be greatly reduced if an American celebrity were along. I let the conversation lapse as I calculated pluses and minuses.

"Jackie, I have to tell you, I'm not real excited about this idea. If it were an appearance *after* the rescue attempt, we might do some good by alerting people to the existence and danger of COG."

"I think Geraldo wants to go along."

"I have no idea where we'll be in Thailand, but almost certainly it will be in a jungle. I can't imagine dragging a camera crew around. Also, I would be very concerned about someone getting hurt, or drawing too much attention, or getting in the way. Frankly, if I'm right about how this goes, I don't think I'll want it on videotape."

Jackie, ever persistent, didn't give up. "I understand," she said, though I didn't think she did. "I've mentioned this to Brad Beckstrom, who agrees that what's most important is recovering the children. But he also sees the benefits if we can expose COG."

"Give me a day to think about it," I said. "We can talk tomorrow."

"God is certainly challenging me with this case," I said to Patti when I got home that night.

"How's that?" she asked.

I told her about Geraldo.

She laughed all the way through dinner. She laughed when we sat down to watch the tube. The giggles continued throughout the evening. I told Patti I was going down to my dojo to think.

I guess it *was* funny, the idea of my lugging a media celebrity around some Far East jungle. When I was with the police department, I felt awkward talking with local reporters. If a national television personality shadowed me, I'd probably freeze up completely.

The idea seemed all wrong to me, a sign of the times, when even the most traumatic and *personal* events are brought live and in color into the nation's living rooms. I could imagine a closeup of Vivian, the distraught mother; zoom in on those confused, tortured kids; get quotes from everybody, the more lurid the better.

My impression of television people envisioned a group that would do what it wanted to when the action began. If I could count on their following my directions, and not their own, it might work. But I didn't suspect for a minute that they'd listen to me.

Part of me really wanted to permit it, though. I hoped it wasn't ego, some previously dormant ham struggling to get out. I didn't know about that. But I knew that I did want the opportunity to demonstrate to the world the evil and ugliness of COG.

Jackie Corey called the next morning, the first of several phone calls I received relating to the missing children that day, and I told her the decision about television belonged to Vivian. I again mentioned the many negatives involved, but said I didn't think any of them were so certain to assure defeat that they should overrule the wishes of the mother.

Brad Beckstrom, another caught up in the plan to expose COG through the media, telephoned to say that ABC's "20/20" had also expressed interest in covering the story. A producer from "20/20" would be calling me.

I heard from her ten minutes later. Alice Pifer talked about the case for an hour, saying all the right words in a manner that rang sincere. She assured me that "20/20" would want to work under my direction—it would be a disaster if we failed because of the show.

I told Alice I couldn't be sure when we would be headed for Thailand, and her reply heartened me. "Whatever time we have," she said, "I can use to research the Children of God."

"How many people will you bring along?" I asked.

"Four in all. Myself, a cameraman, a soundman, and an interpreter."

Vivian chose "20/20" and that was that. Alice Pifer was put on hold, informed that we might leave at any moment. She thus became part of an agonized waiting game that included Mike, Patti, Tanya, and Erica Intravia, Brad Beckstrom, Steve

Haugaard, the parishioners at First Baptist Church, Jackie Corey, the entire staff of Allied Intelligence, and the most anxious of all, Scott Biondo and Vivian Shillander, on the front lines in Thailand.

I did not witness what occurred next. The following account derives from exhaustive reports furnished by Scott Biondo and from numerous conversations with Vivian and Vallop.

On January 16, 1988, Scott and Vivian went to Vallop's magnificent office/residence compound to attend a birthday party for one of Vallop's children. Thai hospitality, a cordial atmosphere, and mouth-watering Asian dishes made the day a memorable one. Scott quickly dismissed from his mind the only possible discordant note: He saw Kasame and Vivian huddled in earnest conversation.

The next day Vallop called Scott at the Ambassador. The Thai's operative in Khon Kaen had talked with a local teacher who had befriended a young girl fitting the description of April Shillander. The teacher said the girl belonged to the Children of God and lived with her father and brothers. The girl had even discussed with the teacher her feelings about "the mother and father being divorced."

The teacher did not know where the girl lived, but believed it was either Khon Kaen or Udon Thani. The girl, very polite and friendly, had said she would return to visit the teacher the next week. Vallop's man had shown the teacher a picture of April, and he said he believed it was the same girl, though the photo was too old for him to make a positive identification.

Scott made the right decision. He started packing for the trip to Khon Kaen.

Scott had Vallop direct his operatives to begin looking for COG houses in Khon Kaen and Udon Thani, which are little towns containing only a few Americans. Neither man thought they would be hard to find in places so small.

He also asked Vallop to be ready to move on Monday morning, January 18, for the six-hour drive through the jungles to within an hour of the Laotian border, where martial law and military skirmishes were daily occurrences. Vallop had law-enforcement contacts who would probably help in both towns.

Vivian was instructed to pack and be prepared for travel the next morning, the plan being for her to remain in the background until the time came to take custody of the children. Once Scott identified them, I would fly to Thailand to direct the recovery and exit the country with the children.

Scott called me on the afternoon of January 17 in Bangkok, about 3 A.M. Sunday morning in St. Louis.

"Mike."

"Who is this?"

"Wake up. I have news."

"Let me guess. You found the children."

"A teacher in Khon Kaen identified April to one of Vallop's investigators. It seems pretty definite. Vallop swears by his man, and it figures they'd be in an out-of-the-way place like that."

"Do you have a house? How about the rest of the children?"

"Nothing yet on a house. And nothing on the Shillander boys. We can only hope they're not off at some brainwashing camp."

"Are you ready to move?"

"We're heading for Khon Kaen tomorrow morning. I'm taking Vallop, Kasame, and another agent, and we'll meet some of Vallop's contacts when we get there. He has people looking for COG houses in both towns."

"What does Vallop say about Khon Kaen and Udon Thani?"

"Very dangerous. The rescue party will be heavily armed. They're mostly policemen and border patrol agents, pretty rough customers, I understand. When do you plan to come?"

"I'll make arrangements and put Terry and Al on standby. I'm going to wait until you get there and evaluate what we have."

"You don't think you should come right away?"

"I first want a confirmed sighting."

"You don't trust that teacher who knows April?"

"I don't trust anyone but you, and I want you to provide the verification. If you spot them, it will be two days at the most before I get there. Maintain surveillance and wait until I arrive.

Remember, we may have only one chance. We have to do it right the first time. And don't forget, I'll have all those television people with me. You need to consider them when you prepare for our arrival. Frankly, I don't know what we're going to do with them."

Like a hungry shark scenting blood, Scott had been in Thailand for two weeks under tremendous pressure and now sensed the denouement.

When I said good-bye to Scott at 3:30 A.M., Patti was wide awake and sitting up in bed.

"I'll go downstairs," I said. "You go back to sleep."

"My curiosity isn't going to let me sleep. I'll make a pot of coffee if you tell me what's going on."

"I think this time I'm really going. Probably in the next day or two," I told her.

"It looks like Scott will find the children," I said, when we'd settled into the living room, each with a steaming cup of coffee.

"That's great, Mike. I'm so happy for you. I wonder what's going through Vivian's mind right now."

"A lot of confusion, probably."

"Why confusion?"

"She hasn't seen those children in more than three years. Patti, they've surely changed a great deal. They look different and think different. They've probably been taught to hate her, and she knows it."

"Are the children in Bangkok?"

"No. In a village just outside," I lied.

"Do I have to tell you not to play Rambo?"

What was this Rambo business? Several others had mentioned it.

"I wouldn't do that," I said. "The competition is too stiff."

"What do you mean by that?"

"The real thing, if that's the way to put it, is already there. Sylvester Stallone is in Thailand right now filming *Rambo III.*"

Patti and I sat and talked for awhile, then woke Tanya and Erica earlier than normal and went to the first mass at St. Joseph's Church.

Later in the morning I called Alice Pifer to update her so she could prepare herself and her crew.

On January 18, 1988, Scott called to say the group had arrived in Khon Kaen and that the operative in that town had already located the COG house and set up a surveillance. I told Scott to work the stakeout if he thought it could be done without being spotted.

There was more good news. The investigator in Udon Thani had located a COG house and a daytime surveillance had been established; nighttime was out—the town was under martial law prohibiting anyone from being outside after sunset. Violators would likely be shot.

I suspected Scott would have a confirmed sighting within the next twenty-four hours. I had my tickets changed again and confirmed for the evening of January 19, with reservations for the twentieth as a backup. I called Alice and told her we would fly out either the nineteenth or twentieth. Travel was coordinated for Alice to fly to St. Louis, then we would go on to Bangkok, where we could catch a flight into the small airport at Khon Kaen on a four-seater commuter plane.

I packed one small bag—the ability to move quickly could prove critical—and almost as an afterthought included a Polaroid camera and film, a precaution in case the children needed passport photos.

Calls were made to Brad Beckstrom in Senator Pressler's office and to Steve Haugaard so they could begin preparations at their end. The prestige and power of a U.S. senator might help us out of a sticky situation, and the Sioux Falls lawyer could be needed for unforeseen legal work.

I placed Terry and Al on a standby team with Don Kissell. Scott, observing the impressive armed might Vallop had mustered, felt we had plenty of backup.

A major fear I'd had from the beginning came back to haunt me as I completed preparations to leave: What if the children had been separated from Richard?

But this worry was far outweighed by Scott's proposed remedy of that possible loophole. If we found the children alone, with Richard away—even on a shopping trip—Vivian could take possession of them. The reason: They were American citizens and Thai courts had not ruled on which parent had custody.

If we found them separated—something we would ardently attempt to arrange—the police would be forced to treat the case as a civil matter. With a power of attorney from Vivian, I'd be within my rights helping her to restrain the children should they try to escape.

We knew how to deal with a civil matter. Long before a COG lawyer could serve her with a subpoena, we would be back safe in the United States.

On January 19, 1988, at 6 A.M., Scott had already set up a discreet surveillance on the suspected Khon Kaen COG house, a typical cult residence surrounded by a high wall. One of Vallop's men had a more visible—and thus better—view of the comings and goings.

It was steamy hot, the beginning of a scorching day, and Scott sweltered in the hidden recesses of a narrow alleyway. He wore Thai clothing but could never pass unnoticed under close inspection.

For five hours he boiled under a sizzling, savage summer sun. The only activity either man observed was the exiting from the COG house of a white male who looked American, in his mid-twenties, who walked out the gate and down the street out of sight.

Scott returned, hungry, thirsty, and hot, to the rundown hotel with its tiny sweatbox rooms (no bathrooms) where he, Vallop, Kasame, and Vivian had spent the night.

About an hour later Scott, Vivian, and Kasame sat in a small restaurant at a table overlooking the sidewalk. Scott noticed a man who appeared to be American walking down the street, and asked Vivian if perchance she recognized him. As she leaned across the table to pick the man out of the crowd, Kasame leaped to his feet and scurried outside, striding toward an individual Scott correctly identified as a COG member.

"What is he doing?" Scott hissed.

"Looks like he's going to talk to the man," Vivian replied calmly. "Maybe he'll learn something."

Scott watched helplessly. He dared not venture outside and be seen. He waited and hoped for the best.

The worst happened. Kasame spoke with the American for a minute or so, and then they began walking toward the restaurant, the Thai investigator pointing in Vivian's direction.

"Stay where you are," Scott said to Vivian, moving quickly to block the door. "If they get by me, walk to the restroom and remain inside."

"Scott," Kasame said, "this man knows of some American children and may be able to help us find them."

Scott said to the COG member, "We're looking for a missing child, who was possibly kidnapped. But I'm sure the youngster isn't here." Out of the corner of his eye he glimpsed Vivian approaching.

"Does he know where my children are?" she asked.

"He doesn't know anything," Scott said. "Let's finish eating."

"If you have any idea where my children are," she said to the COG member, "I want you to tell me right now."

The man asked her name. Scott firmly told Vivian to return to the restaurant, then grabbed the cult member by the arm and walked him down the street.

"She's a mother whose child has possibly been kidnapped," he explained. "Please don't be offended. She has become frantic over the whole affair."

"That's a shame," said the COG man. "I can understand why she is upset."

But the circus continued.

As Scott escorted this potential threat a safe distance down the street, Kasame followed. Scott turned to stop the investigator, but the Thai stepped by him and approached the COG member again, holding out pictures of Vivian and the children.

Scott, trying to appear casual, snatched the photos out of Kasame's hand. He shuffled through them and found one of Vivian and her son Yancha, who was back in the States. He handed it to the COG man, asking if he had seen the child.

Another COG member appeared! He was a young, aggressive type, an American who assumed his friend was being harassed. "What's the problem?" asked the second COG member.

"They're looking for a young boy who has been kidnapped," answered his colleague.

"Who are they?" he asked, his eyes narrowing in suspicion.

"We're helping a lady search for her child," said Scott.

"Who is the woman? What's her name?"

"She's a tourist whose child may have been kidnapped."

"I want to know her name."

"Look, pal, just take a hike. Her name is none of your business."

Scott thanked the first COG member and "suggested" Kasame return with him to the restaurant. They walked side-by-side, but now one of the COG members followed them.

Scott stopped, turned to face the man, and assumed a clearly challenging stance. The man kept coming, a potentially disastrous mistake, demanding to talk to the mother. Scott quickly seized his arm, squeezed it firmly, made it hurt, and hoped no more muscle would be required.

"Look," Scott said, "I have a lady who is extremely upset about losing her child. I don't want her disturbed any more. She simply asked your friend if he had seen the child. Now butt out. Get lost!"

"All right! I thought I might help. It's what Jesus Christ would have wanted me to do."

The COG members left and Scott guided Kasame back into the restaurant. Vivian was waiting inside.

"What did he tell you?" Vivian wanted to know.

"What's the matter with you and Kasame?" Scott countered.

"I am sorry, Scott," Kasame said. "I wanted to help find the children quickly. I was not going to tell them who we really are."

"You don't think they could figure that out if you showed them a picture of the children? And you, Vivian! You, better than anyone, should know what will happen if COG finds out about us."

Vivian sighed and said in a defeated voice, "I know. I couldn't help it. It's driving me up the wall thinking that the children may be around the next corner, and I'm sitting here like a lump, doing nothing."

"This could alert the whole COG community," Scott said. "They'll know something's wrong."

Kasame's ego and concern for the children had caused him to make a serious mistake. However, a second cooler-headed Thai investigator had held his position outside the restaurant and did not expose himself. When Scott left with

Vivian and Kasame, the investigator made sure the trio wasn't followed.

Scott returned to his hotel room, anxious about Kasame and Vivian. Kasame had jeopardized the case and would likely have revealed identities if Scott hadn't reacted quickly. His thoughts were interrupted by a knock on his door. It was Vallop.

"We have found them!" the Thai announced.

"At the house here in Khon Kaen?"

"No. They are in Udon Thani, at the residence we have been watching there."

"How many of the children were seen?"

"My man talked to April and John."

"What do you mean, 'talked to them'?"

"He went to the house asking for work and spoke with April and John. They said their father would be home later and that their mother did not live with them. No adults were in the house. This investigator has a copy of the picture you sent me and is sure they are the Shillander children."

"How far away is Udon Thani?"

"We must drive maybe one hour over very bad roads. It is near Laos, and we must be careful because it is dangerous there. The area is near provinces under total martial law; we cannot go at night."

"We should leave at daybreak tomorrow."

"I will tell Kasame and let my police friends know we are coming. We should get the children and leave right away."

"Let me call Mike. He'll come over and be in charge of the recovery and getting them home safely."

"Okay, Scott. I will get ready."

Wisely, Scott had not overreacted to Kasame's blunder. He was close now, too close to risk friction. Even if Vivian and Kasame had not exposed us (Scott hoped he had managed to cover up the mistake), he needed her for the recovery. By law, she had to be present to take custody of the kids.

Scott called and told me about the Kasame-COG incident and that Vallop's investigator had talked with April and John. My irritation with Vivian and Kasame quickly dissipated as we discussed locating and recovering the children.

Scott worried about holding the investigation together until I got there. Vivian, Kasame, even Vallop, had grown impatient. Her disappointments over the past three years, plus physical stress, and loneliness had broken her heart and she gravitated toward what she conceived to be the shortest path to her children.

"Stay strong," I urged Scott. "Get more forceful with Vivian if you have to. She's like a person drowning—kicking, screaming, and lashing out at the people trying to save her. At least Vallop's located two of the children. Most likely the other two will return to the house with Richard."

"When will you be here?"

"Go to Udon Thani in the morning. As soon as you positively identify the children as Vivian's, I'll be in the air."

I had faith in Scott, but his best—or anybody else's— might not be enough to prevent another incident. Once he identified the children, he would have to stake out the house, using the Thai investigators, and stay with Vivian until I could get there. It would be a long two days for the young detective.

▲
Scott Biondo &
Kasame in the ve
used to transport
children.

10

The Worst
Possible Move

THE NEXT DAY, WEDNESDAY, JANUARY 20, I arrived in the office at 6 A.M., prepared to leave the country. It was 8 P.M. Thursday in Udon Thani, and I suspected Scott had not yet sighted the children. I had instructed him to call as soon as he identified them, or to call Friday before noon. I held tickets for flights Wednesday, Thursday, and Friday, and had brought my passport and suitcase to the office.

Around the globe, at that moment, Scott listened to the clank and roar of armored military vehicles patrolling the streets of Udon Thani as he left the surveillance team that blended into the scenery around the COG house. He rented three rooms in a nearby ancient hotel and planted Vivian in one of them, giving her strict orders not to leave. He returned to the stakeout periodically to maintain tight control over the Thai investigators. They observed a white man and woman leave the COG house and return later in the afternoon, but by the end of the day, the children had not been spotted.

The temperature soaring over 100 degrees, murderous humidity, and long, stressful hours completely exhausted Scott. He went to bed early.

About 11 P.M., a loud explosion jarred him awake, followed by others close enough to rattle the windows in his room. War raged in Udon Thani.

He had just fallen asleep again when, at 1 A.M., the telephone woke him on the first ring.

"Scott, were you sleeping?" It was Vivian.

"Not soundly. What is it?"

"I'm confused. I talked to Kasame and the other investigators earlier, and they think we should go to the house and get the children—stop all this playing around."

"*Playing* around!" he said sharply, then checked his temper and softened his tone. "I know how you must feel, Vivian, but please, just trust us a little longer. We've come too far to take a chance of ruining everything."

"We know the children are in that house. It seems crazy to wait."

"Vivian, we don't know. We're perhaps 85 percent sure, and another day or two to make certain won't hurt. Besides, taking custody of your children is only half of the work; getting them out of the country and home will be just as difficult. It may be as easy as going up to the house, recovering them, returning to Bangkok, and catching a plane out. But it rarely goes that smoothly. I have to remind you again: If you blow our cover, you may never lay eyes on those children again."

"All right. Forget what I said and go back to sleep. Sorry to have bothered you."

"No bother. That's one of the reasons I'm here."

"This is just so hard for me, but talking about it really helps. Thanks, Scott. I'll see you in the morning and pray that you spot the children then."

Scott knew if he did identify the kids, he would have to camp out on Vivian's doorstep to keep her from heading straight for them too soon. He emphasized to Vallop *not* to follow any order issued by Vivian.

She called again at 4:30 A.M.

"Scott, I'm not going to argue or even discuss this with you. I've thought about it all night, and I've talked with the Thais. They've agreed to take me to get my children at daybreak."

"Please. Don't! You're making a terrible mistake."

"We're leaving at six. Scott, I'd like for you to come, but I suppose you won't disobey Mike's orders."

"This is the worst possible move, Vivian."

"I won't wait any longer."

"I'll go with you. I can't let you go alone."

Scott knew he couldn't stop her, and if they did recover the children, he would have his work cut out getting them back to the States.

Vallop went along with the move because his investigators believed it would work, and Vivian wanted it done. He estimated the danger would be minimal since he had friends on the police department to protect them. The police would also conduct a passport and visa inspection—something within the realm of their authority—separating the children from the adults. That would allow Vivian to take custody.

The sun rose and lifted the curfew, but it didn't brighten Scott's dark thoughts.

He compared the Thai investigators to mutineers. Vivian's anxiety and the Thais' egos had conspired overwhelmingly against us. The Thais wanted to show the distressed mother their sincere compassion, and their ability in Thailand to recover children without the supervision of an American overseer.

Quiet pervaded the short drive to the COG house. A motorcade of three cars pulled up in front of the residence, and the police strategically took places at the rear and front.

Everyone was armed and moved quickly. Scott remained in the car with Vivian. Vallop, Kasame, and the police approached the door.

One of the COG members awakened and came to see what caused the ruckus outside. He was immediately overpowered, and law-enforcement officers went from room to room securing the residence and herding occupants to the front.

Vivian swayed back and forth in her seat, trying for a better view of the youngsters exiting the house.

"Hold your horses," Scott said. "Wait until they've separated Richard from the children."

"I can't stand this. Please, God, return them. Please, God, answer this one prayer."

"Stay calm, Vivian."

"Oh, my God! Look! It's April!" she screamed.

Vivian jumped out of the car like an Olympic sprinter leaving the blocks, and went running forward, crying "April!"

As Scott raced to catch up with Vivian, they both realized the girl was not April. Vivian looked around frantically, then began to wail.

"Get back in the car," Scott ordered. "The police may have them inside, trying to separate them from Richard."

The command went unheeded.

Vivian *knew* her children were there, and she confronted some of the COG people undergoing passport inspection. "Tell me where my children are!" she demanded from a COG man. She grabbed the arm of a female cultist and asked, "Do you know April?" Whirling herself around in a circle of puzzled faces, Vivian finally tilted her head skyward and screamed, "Oh, God! Give me back my babies!"

Scott put his arm tightly around Vivian's shoulders and tried to reason with her, but none of his words could reach her now. He slowly inched her back toward the car.

Vallop and the investigator who had talked with "April" and "John" approached Vivian. When they pointed out the boy and girl the investigator had spoken with and assumed were her children, she could see why he had falsely identified them as hers. They were the same ages, had the same hair color, and, unbelievably, the same names. But they were not Vivian's children.

It was an incredible collection of coincidences: four children, including an April and a John, and a father, all American members of COG. It all added up to an understandable mistake on the part of the Thai investigator.

The scene unraveled badly. One of the COG men came over to Vivian and asked, "Who are you? What do you want?"

"I want to know where the Shillander children are. Tell me, or you're going to be in bad trouble."

"Who are you?"

"Get away from her," Scott told him.

"I'm their mother, and I have a right to know."

Another COG man approached, asking the same questions, demanding to know Vivian's name and what she wanted.

"I'm Vivian Shillander. I want my children."

"Vivian!" Scott ordered. "Get back in the car right now!"

He looked into her sad, glazed eyes. Despairing eyes. Scott finally got her inside, and Vallop sat next to her. A COG member, unbelievably, tried to climb in with them.

"Where are *you* going?" Scott demanded.

"I want to know what's happening. Why is this woman looking for her children here?"

"Get away from us."

Another COG male headed for Vivian. Scott moved behind him, grabbed his left arm and the back of his collar, and jerked him almost to the ground.

"Your persistence is going to get you hurt," Scott said through clenched teeth.

Generally, COG men are nonviolent and these two had been around the block enough times to know they were in over their heads. It took no message from Moses David Berg to tell them they faced an angry, dangerous man.

The drive back to Bangkok resembled a small funeral procession. Dead were the excitement and promises of a new life for Vivian and her children; that hope was buried in the front yard of a COG house in Udon Thani.

Vivian condemned COG for keeping the children from her. Vallop and Kasame made profuse apologies. Scott didn't want to hear any of it.

A few hours after Vivian had been ensconced at the Baptist Guest House, she came out of the fog and began to see things more clearly.

"I'm sorry I didn't listen to you, Scott."

"We can talk about it later."

"Are you mad at me?"

"I'm not happy. But I understand."

"God help me. I've probably lost them forever."

Vivian shed many tears over the next few days, and it was impossible for anyone to remain angry with her for mistakes all too human, stemming from a mother's love and concern.

When I heard the news of the fiasco from Scott, my mind teetered on the edge of despair. I had lived the frustrations of this case almost every waking hour for more than half a year, and now feared we had blown it. From the beginning I had engineered all efforts around a single premise: a one-shot chance at recovering the four young Shillanders. The Children of God's communication network now would warn Richard, and he would split the country. Years could pass before we had another chance. It might never happen at all.

By the time Vivian called to explain and apologize, I found it impossible to berate this grief-stricken mother. She agreed that Richard would soon learn about what had happened in the Udon Thani house search and leave the country within minutes. I believed Vallop's Thai Immigration contacts would stop Richard if he left through normal channels, but the COG would surely facilitate his exodus through an irregular border checkpoint.

I gave Vivian two alternatives: (1) Return to the United States and continue using the Thai investigators in the hope they would obtain a *confirmed* sighting; or (2) I would come to Thailand and make an all-out last push with hand-selected operatives penetrating the jungle to flush out COG people in an attempt to pinpoint Richard's whereabouts. I would try to bluff them. Our company had done it before, rescuing those children from Mexico and Peru.

Vivian opted for the second choice.

I felt as though I had just come off an operating table, all my energy drained. I had been packed and ready to leave, watching every revolution the minute hand made on my office clock, and wasn't prepared for these developments. I had suspected this could happen, but always dismissed these thoughts as overly negative thinking.

I tried to put myself in Richard's shoes. What would he do? No matter how many times I posed the question, the answer always came back the same: flee Thailand.

But something kept nagging at me. I tried again to get a handle on Richard.

This man had remained safe and undisturbed for years. Why hadn't he left Thailand long ago? He probably liked the country, and had possibly become attached to someone or something that kept him there.

Would he pack up and take the children away immediately? Maybe not. Maybe what kept him there exercised a strong hold. He might also, I hoped, feel false security because he had lived in Thailand for so long.

Then I thought of that January 28 visa renewal for the children, our forgotten ace in the hole. A long shot, but better than no shot at all.

I made arrangements to fly out on January 24, 1988, with "20/20"'s Alice Pifer along. A freelance cameraman, stationed in the Philippines, would join us in Thailand, and the soundman and interpreter would be native Thais employed by ABC. I emphasized, and Alice fully understood, that our chance of finding the children was now very slim.

At St. Louis' Lambert Field, my wife and daughters waited with me as the big 747 taxied onto the tarmac and took on fuel for the transoceanic flight. Patti harbored worrisome visions of pipe-wielding muggers, back-stabbing thieves, and dime-a-dozen hitmen lurking in the shadowy recesses of Bangkok. Tanya and Erica bubbled the naiveté of seeing off their conquering hero father.

"You will find the kids for their mom, won't you, Dad?" Tanya asked.

"I hope so, Honey. Say a prayer for us."

"I will. Tell Scott we said hello."

"I hope you find them, too," said Erica. "You're not going to get hurt, are you?"

"No, Sweetheart. Don't worry. I'll be back soon."

Patti looked at me and pursed her lips. She reached over and squeezed my hand.

Kasame and other
employees and friends
of Vallops at the party
Scott and Vivian
attended.

◀ Kasame, Alice, and
crew member waiting
on the parking lot.

11

An Unholy Alliance

THE BIG ALUMINUM AIRSHIP JETTED US high above the waters of the Pacific, crossed the International Dateline into a new day, descended over miles of rice paddies in Thailand's central plains, and touched down north of Bangkok at Don Maung Airport.

I advanced my watch to Thai time—10:30 P.M., January 25, 1988—and stretched muscles that felt atrophied after thirty hours of limited movement. I'd spent the entire trip briefing Alice Pifer, dozing, and thinking about the nation I was about to visit, so different from my own.

Thailand was the only country in Southeast Asia that had never served time as a colony of one or another European power. Its name was, until 1939, Siam, a Sanskrit word meaning "green" or "gold." The present name translates in English to "land of the free," and the form of government is a "constitutional" monarchy, though in reality the military holds the power. Archaeologists declare a sophisticated culture existed here that predates even the Chinese.

Green is still an appropriate word to describe this beautiful place; it is as green as Ireland. The color covers its fields, mountains, and jungles. More than 80 percent of the nation is agrarian—Thailand is one of the most fertile rice bowls in the world—and the dominant religion is Buddhism.

Most Americans know about Thailand, if they know about it at all, from *Anna and the King of Siam* (originally, *An English Governess in the Court of Siam*) and from Pierre Boulle's

Bridge over the River Kwai, describing the "Death Railway"
POWs built there during World War II.

Scott waved as I got off the plane, and a Thai ABC employee greeted Alice Pifer.

The thick, damp, tropical smell of the air made breathing
uncomfortable. It is usually hot in Thailand, but this was the
dead of summer. Other than the airline losing my single suitcase, I was glad to be here: optimistic, despite the grim reality,
and eager to get cracking.

Our two groups piled into separate cars and got on the
Bagna-Port Expressway, a new road opened in 1962 that runs
south directly to the coast and the beautiful beaches on the
Gulf of Siam. We exited the expressway, which goes *over*
Bangkok, and headed to the Ambassador Hotel, near the busy
center of the city.

During the twelve-mile ride, Scott highlighted the three-
plus weeks since his arrival. "Vallop," he said, "has helped me
put all the passport control points on alert to notify us if
Richard and the children try to leave the country. However, as
you know, some checkpoints are so far out in the boondocks it
will take weeks for the message to get back here. But assuming
Richard intends to stay in the country, it's stamped on the papers that he'll have to renew the visas on January 28 at the
Immigration building in Bangkok."

"What if he comes in early?"

"It won't do him any good. The clerks at Immigration will
tell him to return on the scheduled date. We have that base
covered."

"Good," I said, as the butterflies in my stomach punctu-
ated my thoughts of January 28, which "20/20" narrator Tom
Jarriel later would describe as "a day of awesome possibilities."
I had less than three days to position all my people.

"Mike," Scott said, and then hesitated as our car zipped
down the expressway toward Bangkok.

"What is it?" I glanced at Scott and saw that the next news
wouldn't be good.

"Well, we've counted on the visa renewal as our ace in the
hole, but Richard may have a more powerful trick up his sleeve."

"What are you saying?"

"Possibly Richard, Mr. Nonviolent, may have managed to tie himself in with an army colonel by the name of Thu Lee who is assigned to one of the border areas."

"What do you know about him?"

"My profile on this guy shows him as ruthless and deadly, with the reputation of killing anybody who gets in his way—rules like a warlord, a description he thoroughly fits."

I learned that even the prominent, influential Vallop, though he remained in our corner, had a healthy fear of Colonel Thu Lee. And some of his investigators, hearing about Thu Lee's possible involvement, had already backed out of the case. They said if Thu Lee learned about our search for the Shillander children, he would order his troops to shoot us and leave our bodies to rot in the jungle.

No one knew Richard's exact relationship with Colonel Thu Lee, but the specter of Thu Lee, a savage, powerful enemy, added a dimension of danger I hadn't imagined in my wildest scenarios.

Downtown Bangkok hadn't changed; it was still a place of chaos. Its name means City of Angels, and six million people reside there, most of them in poverty, amid a boomtown vitality of hustling and wheeling-dealing.

I checked into the Ambassador Hotel, where Scott stayed, and it became our base of operations. The Ambassador, the largest hotel in Thailand, features a thousand rooms, including many suites, plus attractive grounds and several fine restaurants: Hong Teh Cantonese, Tokugawa Japanese, and the Dickens Pub. We couldn't have known at the time, but the penultimate scene in the Shillander drama would play out at the Ambassador.

Scott and I were up and ready to work at 9 A.M. on January 26, meeting over coffee in the Café Ambassador to coordinate activities over the next few crucial days.

"Scott," I said, "I was so tired last night and spaced out with jet lag that I failed to tell you what a good job you've done in the face of terrific obstacles."

"I appreciate it. You were right on the money when you predicted I'd have problems. I didn't think they'd be to this degree, though."

"Neither did I."

"Do you really think we have much of a chance to find the children? I was surprised when you decided to come at this time."

"Yes. I think we have a chance, though maybe not a very good one. I believe it's possible Richard's been in Thailand so long he's developed a feeling of invulnerability. It might even be merited, given that possible unholy alliance with Thu Lee. For sure, *something's* keeping him here. Maybe he's accumulated money and is having trouble smuggling it out. Maybe he's re-married. Whatever, we start that job in Europe on February 3, and it behooves us to accomplish what we can now. No telling when we'll be able to get back to this case, which by any measure is our most important."

"It's interesting, isn't it, after all the searching? The mountain may actually come to Mohammed."

"More like tracking an animal. The trail peters out, and when you're about to give up the hunt, the animal comes to you."

"What if he doesn't?"

"If he doesn't, we'll still have a few days before Europe. We'll go to Udon Thani, Khon Kaen, and any COG settlements we can find here in Bangkok. You and I will talk to the residents and see if we can't convince them it's in everyone's best interest for Vivian to recover her children."

"What about the people from ABC?"

"I like Alice Pifer. She's done her homework. We had a good, long talk on the plane, and I believe she's sincere in her willingness to take our direction."

"Speaking of direction," Scott said with a grin, "it's time for 'lights, camera, action,' Mr. Intravia."

Scott was referring to my first meeting with Vivian. She had arrived early at the Ambassador and been interviewed by Alice Pifer, and now they waited to tape a client-meets-investigator segment for the report.

Conducting our initial face-to-face session under the revealing, up-close-and-personal eye of a television camera would have been awkward under any circumstances, and this morning I felt particularly self-conscious about my appearance. The airline hadn't found my luggage and, except for a clean shirt borrowed from Scott, I wore the same clothes I'd left St. Louis in.

In a conference room of the Ambassador, the film crew had set up their equipment in front of a couch and chairs positioned in a talk show arrangement. Scott and I, feeling like fools, walked down an aisle toward Vivian, determined to get it over with quickly so we could get back to business.

Vivian looked exactly as I had imagined. Small, pretty, her eyes haunted. She started to shake my hand, then moved to hug me, then pulled back. We sat down stiffly and the television people attached lavaliere microphones to our clothing.

"Mike, it's nice to finally meet you," Vivian said. "I'm glad you're here."

"So am I."

"Okay," announced Alice Pifer. "We're ready. I want to thank you for cooperating, Mike. I know you have a lot to do in a short time. Just pretend we aren't here. Go ahead and have your meeting."

"Vivian," I said, "how are you feeling?"

"Defeated. Things don't seem to be working out. I know our chances are slim, but I've prayed hard on this. I just can't go back home to Sioux Falls without my children."

This was unnatural and embarrassing for both of us. Through our many phone conversations I felt I'd gotten to know Vivian, identify with her, and this struck me as a ridiculous personal introduction. Still, we were trapped, with nothing to do but carry on.

"We need to talk about what will happen in the next few days. I know how tired you are. Are you sure you're going to be strong enough for this?"

"Except for being horribly depressed, I have all the strength I'll need."

"Good. If we find the children, they'll be very confused and need a strong, healthy mother to lean on."

"I'll be okay. I just hope we find them."

"Scott and I will be doing a lot of legwork over the next few days, setting the stage for Thursday when Richard's supposed to renew the visas at Immigration. I'm banking on Thursday. Between now and then we'll develop the specific role you need to play."

"What do you mean, 'role'?"

"You'll have to be available to take custody of your children and afterward to take care of them. Don't worry yourself with anything else between now and then; Scott and I will handle all the details. I want you to concentrate on two things: taking custody of your family, and keeping them safe."

Suddenly there was a commotion, and a member of the crew shouted, "Cut! Quick! Douse the lights!"

"What's the matter?" Alice Pifer wanted to know.

"The ceiling's on fire!" shouted the lighting technician.

Intense heat from a studio light had melted a large plastic ceiling panel which now hung down over the "set" and temporarily halted production. Alice called the hotel manager, promising that ABC would pay for the damage, and we talked while workmen made repairs.

Alice and Vivian had hit it off from the start. The peppy, attractive newswoman in her mid-thirties was truly impressed by Vivian's suffering under the double-edged sword of the COG. When fourteen years of whittling away at the independence of a once-idealistic college student failed to sculpt a satisfactorily submissive indentured servant of Moses David Berg, the cult in one fell swoop severed Vivian's soul by separating her from the children. Alice, more than a reporter covering an assignment, hung on every word as Vivian recounted life in the cult. Later, Alice would work hard at revealing the horrors of the Children of God to the American public. She, like the rest of us, became committed to Vivian's recovery cause.

I believed Alice and Vivian would be good company for each other, and I welcomed their relationship, which would free me to get everything in place for Thursday.

As soon as someone announced, "It's a wrap," Scott and I hurried from the conference room, knowing we had only two days left to salvage the investigation.

Outside the hotel we made an assessment of the traffic flow and decided to take a cab to our first stop. Bangkok used to be called the "Venice of the East" because of its canal network. Depending on the hour, travelers can often make better time by going the old-fashioned way, using a water taxi, to avoid the world-famous traffic jams.

When our cab delivered us to the American Embassy, Scott and I stepped into a crowd of people milling around out front.

We squeezed our way through to the gate and told the Marine security guard that we had an appointment with Ed Wehrli, the American consul.

Ten minutes later a tall, distinguished-looking man in his early forties picked us out of the masses and led us through security checkpoints to his office where he made sure we were comfortable.

"Have you been to Thailand before, Mike?" Wehrli asked.

"Yes, not long ago. It's a fascinating country."

"I've met with Vivian Shillander, as I'm sure you know. I tried to explain to her that there's not a lot I can do, but I'll help whatever way I can . . . legally." He let the word hang in the air. "Personally, I hope you find the children and take them home. What you want to accomplish, however, can inflame some very sensitive nerves. I hope you understand what I'm saying."

"I appreciate your situation. I assure you we intend to operate within the law."

"That's what I hoped to hear. We can't tolerate mercenary, break-down-the-door operations, regardless of how appealing they might be. Still, its terrible to think of those children trapped in that cult for the rest of their lives."

"Yes, it is."

"You know, don't you, that the Children of God were kicked out of the Philippines, and many of them were arrested for running a prostitution business?"

"I heard about it. Richard Shillander was in the Philippines when it happened."

"Well, how can I be of help?"

"What if we recover the children and can't find their passports? Will we have problems getting new ones? I assume Vivian showed you the court documents giving her custody of the children."

"Yes, I think we can accommodate new passports under these circumstances. And no, I didn't see those papers."

"They were signed by a South Dakota judge."

"Not the weightiest legal authority I've ever heard of," he sighed. "But we work with what we have. I assume you'll want to leave the country as soon as you have the children, so you don't get caught up in civil or criminal confrontations."

"That's exactly what I intend."

In the back seat of a taxi that lacked air conditioning, our clothes clinging to us like sodden tissue paper, the humidity oppressive and the sun scorching our brains to dust, Scott and I waited in a monumental traffic jam breathing exhaust fumes spewed from rickety motorcycles, Bangkok's least expensive and thus most popular mode of transportation. As many as five people often straddle a single bike and move between the grid-locked automobiles.

Our driver dropped us at Immigration after a remarkable thirty minutes, employing amazing evasive driving skills to counter the horrendous traffic conditions. The man would have been great on our side of the law in a moving surveillance situation, or on the other side making a getaway.

I smiled at the analogy. *We* might soon be the ones making the getaway.

The Immigration building stood in the heart of Bangkok, a big stone structure with a small plaza where people sat on the grass eating lunch.

Scott and I walked the perimeter of the building, making sure the only way in was the front entrance. Trees and alleys surrounded the building, with space to park in the rear, but to get inside, a person had to enter through the front.

Three Thai men worked on a car at the end of a trashcan-lined alley along the side of the Immigration building. The noise of the city was terrific, so I didn't hear right away the growling of two large mongrel dogs who had come charging out of a small shack.

We started to run, Scott grabbing a lid off a trashcan. I saw a broom propped against the side of a building, broke it in half, and turned to face the dogs. There was no way we could outrun them; standing to fight offered the only solution. Scott smashed the lid into the face of one dog, knocking it backward. I had broken the broom to create a weapon similar to one I practice with, and jabbed at the second animal.

The dog snarled and snapped, showing sharp, yellow teeth. Down the alley we heard the Thai workers laughing, enjoying the show, at the moment not an amusing one to us.

Scott's dog charged again and once more he struck it full in the face with the trashcan lid. "My" dog lunged toward my throat with a mighty leap, and I hit him in mid-air with full force, probably breaking his nose. He turned and ran crying, and the second dog simply quit growling and barking and followed his accomplice.

"Great," I said. "We almost spent the next month recovering from rabies."

"I wonder if the dogs belong to those workers."

We looked down the alley and saw them bent over in laughter.

"I doubt it. But I'll bet you and I aren't the only ones who have given them a good show."

"Well," Scott said, "I'm not fond of fighting dogs. I'd much rather have been jumped by those guys."

We laughed, exiting the alley, found a taxi, and visited hotels where Berg's Flirty Fishers might be working. We struck out in this department—it was probably too early in the day—but more importantly I had obtained a good picture of how to stakeout the Immigration building on January 28.

My clothes were shot. We had the driver drop us at a mall, where I bought a suit, hoping my luggage would arrive that evening. We had arranged to go out to dinner with Vivian, Alice Pifer, and one of the television crew members. I knew just the spot for good Asian seafood and felt everyone could benefit from a haven of calm before the storm struck.

▲
Scott & Vivian on
Guest House grounds.

12

Tackling the Bureaucracy— and Others

JANUARY 27, 1988. Before sunrise I was out of bed and waiting for the city to wake up. My hotel room, small by American standards, had enough space for a light workout. I bore down in hard martial arts concentration to obtain the best mindset for tackling the final preparations of the recovery. The contacts and strategies developed today could make the difference between success or failure if Richard and the children showed up tomorrow at Immigration.

After I showered, shaved, and dressed in the clothes purchased the previous afternoon, I asked Scott if he was ready to get started.

"Yeah. I'm raring to go."

"Me too, but none of the people we have to see are at work yet."

"How about breakfast at the floating market?"

"Good idea. We'll kill some time before Vallop's man gets here, and grab a breath of fresh air before all the engines get revved up."

Rivers and klongs (canals) are a vital part of life in Thailand. For more than four centuries the heart of Siam, Ayuthaya, sat on an artificial island in the mighty Chao Phraya River and was crisscrossed by a network of klongs. In 1872, when the capital moved to Bangkok, a similar canal system was built.

Several generations of farmers supported their families by paddling homegrown meat and produce into the city to sell and trade. But when Bangkok developed as the crossroads of Southeast Asia, floating markets for tourists were restricted to the Wat Sai, across the Chao Phraya from Bangkok, and another a few miles upriver.

Scott and I, much ahead of the rush hour madness, made it to the floating market at Wat Sai in record time and found the canals covered with sampans overflowing with lush fruits (mangoes, bananas, pineapples, apples, and berries), rice sacks, whole sides of beef and pork, dried fish, and bouquets of beautiful tropical blossoms.

We filled our stomachs with fresh-off-the-tree fruits and our senses with the unforgettable smells, sounds, and sights of locals sitting cross-legged in the bottoms of wall-to-wall sampans hawking their wares from beneath wide-brimmed straw hats, which come to a point on top and resemble lamp shades.

We got back to the Ambassador a few minutes before a driver arrived to take us to Vallop's office. Vallop heads a very large security operation: for his thousands of employees (St. Louis and Kansas City combined do not have this many police officers), he even owns a bus company to transport them to and from work, a laundry to clean their uniforms, and a cafeteria to feed them.

As we approached the perimeter of the sprawling compound where his home and business are located, it resembled a prison camp guarded by armed men. But inside the walls a splendid home, huge courtyard, and lush tropical garden sprawled before us.

The receptionist, a young, pretty Thai woman with long, black hair, bowed as she greeted us. She led us to Vallop's office, and we removed our shoes before entering.

His formal office sparkled like a meticulously arranged showroom of an exclusive Thai furniture company. Red and green hand-tied Oriental area rugs colored the polished hardwood floor, a massive desk carved from native teak wood—one of Thailand's chief exports—filled one corner. In another corner, a couch and chairs were arranged around a glass-top bamboo table for entertaining clients. Swords gleamed on the walls, and a large glass curio cabinet contained ancient Asian statues.

The focal point of the office was an altar to Buddha decorated with the warm glow of burning candles and fragrant flowers from the garden.

Vallop rose from his chair, as did Kasame and Captain Pradaphit. Pradaphit, a Thai police captain who worked part-time for Vallop, had asked to meet his associates from America. The Thais made traditional bows, with their palms pressed together as in prayer, in front of their chests. This is called a *wai* and Thais are flattered when Westerners return the polite gesture, which Scott and I did. Then we gave them an American handshake.

"It is so good to see you, my friend," Vallop said. "I hope your trip was pleasant."

"Yes," I said. "It was fine, and I'm happy to be in Bangkok again."

Vallop introduced Kasame and Captain Pradaphit, and invited everyone to join him for a drink. His secretary served us refreshing tropical fruit concoctions in tall, chilled glasses.

I complimented our host by admiring his impressive desk.

"I found it in a northern province," Vallop said, "and had it shipped down on a river barge. Almost half of Thailand is covered with forests and lumber is a big business. It is interesting that in the old days elephants were used in forestry. Now most everything is machines. But on difficult ground elephants still move the large tree trunks."

After more polite conversation on matters of no importance, I brought up the purpose of our visit. "We need to discuss tomorrow, and the plans I've made."

"It does not seem this Richard will show up," Vallop said. "He is probably gone now."

"You may be right," I said. "If he is still here and doesn't come to renew the children's visas, will he be arrested?"

"I doubt it," said Captain Pradaphit. "It is against the law, but not so bad, and Immigration will not arrest."

"What will you do if Richard does not come?" Vallop asked me.

"With your help, I would like to go to the COG houses in Khon Kaen, Udon Thani, and Bangkok and speak with the residents."

"I do not think they will talk."

"Maybe. Maybe not. Perhaps I can find the right words to convince them to tell us what we want to know. If not, my friend, Scott and I will return to Thailand at a later date, hoping you will continue to help us."

"It would be a pleasure. I hope the previous confusion in Khon Kaen and Udon Thani does not hurt you."

"There has been damage, Vallop. But we must forget."

"Your Scott, he is good investigator," said Vallop. Four sets of eyes turned toward Scott and I noticed his face flush as Vallop continued. "We should have listened to him, but we were confused because Vivian told us to get the children from the house now. She is paying us, and tells us this."

"I understand. Please, next time, remember you are working for me. When you are in the United States with a case, we will listen to you. The clients are not investigators, and we must do what is right."

"These are good words. I hope some day to come to the United States and work with you."

I had no intention of rehashing the problems in Khon Kaen or Udon Thani, but Vallop's broaching the subject released some of the tension. Vallop made Vivian the heavy, while she claimed Kasame had talked her into going after the children and not waiting for the "big boss" from the United States. It made no sense now to try to distribute blame.

We discussed Thursday's strategy, beginning with a 7 A.M. surveillance at the Immigration office. The building opened at 8, and I would take no chances of missing Richard. Scott would be stationed in the waiting area at the main entrance. I would be positioned on the second floor outside the office where Americans renew visas. Vivian would be in a van on the parking lot with Alice Pifer and the camera crew.

In addition to the van with dark, tinted one-way windows, I needed two more surveillance vehicles: a motorcycle posted at the rear of the building, whose driver could easily maneuver through heavy traffic, and a car at the front with a driver assigned to me.

I figured Richard would not bring the children, although I hoped he would. If he did come alone, I had to arrange for Immigration to insist that he take an officer to his house.

However, if he brought one or two of the kids, we would need another vehicle to begin immediately hunting down the others before COG members had a chance to hide them.

Vallop's friend at Immigration had arranged to be notified when Richard arrived for the paperwork. As a Thai Immigration investigator, he would usher Richard upstairs and interrogate him for violating Thai law by not reporting his new address when he moved there. While the children (if he brought them) were left unattended, Vivian could legally take custody of them and leave to avoid a confrontation with her estranged husband. I would serve Richard with the legal documents from the South Dakota court regarding custody, divorce, and an order of protection. Then I would catch up with Vivian and the children and hop a flight that evening for the United States.

I had not met the Thai Immigration contact, but I felt confident the plan would work if Richard brought the children. A Thai regulation required him to produce them; however, it was not strictly enforced, and he would not likely know about the law.

Vallop said he would come to the Immigration office on January 28, but couldn't stay the entire day. It was clear he did not want to waste time on a surveillance he felt would be unsuccessful.

He promised to have two of his agents present and added, "I do not think Kasame will be one." I had not asked him to leave out Kasame. Vallop made the decision, trying to avoid any embarrassment.

It heartened me that Vallop and the others were friendly. They praised Scott and his abilities. Despite all the problems, Scott had managed not to overreact in Khon Kaen and Udon Thani, and maintained a good relationship with the Thais, as well as their respect.

Scott and I bowed as we left the office, and Vallop's chauffeur drove us through brain-boggling confusion to the Immigration office.

I told a policeman guarding the front door that I needed to see Investigator Ayuthaya (an easy name to remember, spelled exactly like Thailand's old capital). The officer verified that we were expected, and directed us up four flights of steps.

The old building had tile floors and twelve-foot ceilings. The windows in the corridors were open, allowing in fresh air, since the structure had no air conditioning.

We finally found the inspector's office where Ayuthaya worked. Ayuthaya bowed to greet us. I guessed his age at thirty-five. He had brown skin, dark black hair combed to the side and back, and the very warm, gentle smile common to most Thais. Investigators and secretaries kept giving us double takes, apparently intrigued by the presence of American visitors.

Ayuthaya had been one of the people helping us from the beginning, and I started the conversation by thanking him as graciously as I could.

"It is okay," he said. "I always do favor for my friend. Vallop is my friend, so I do favor for you. It is an honor to do for you. Please excuse me, my English is not so good."

"Your English is good," I said, "and much better than my Thai. Has Vallop called and explained what we need tomorrow?"

"Yes, Vallop calls. This may be difficult. I must have reason to begin investigation. Do you know what I say?"

"Yes. But there *is* a reason: Richard Shillander has broken Thai Immigration law. He has not given you a correct address. He does not live where he says. Wrong address is against Thai law, yes?"

"I must have proof to go to my captain. He must begin investigation, and then I have authority."

"Ayuthaya, can you have an investigator go to the house Richard reports as his residence? The investigator can see that he has moved."

"Yes, I can do this."

He talked to a fellow investigator, then told us the man, who smiled, bowed, and left, would check out Richard's former house.

"Can we see the forms for reentering Thailand that Richard Shillander completed when he returned from his trips?" I asked.

"Yes," he said, "I can find them. We must go to another building and see my friend. I ask him to do us favor."

Ayuthaya led us out of Immigration and down an alley to another building, a warehouse where Immigration Department documents were stored. Computers had not yet been interfaced with many of the government offices, and Immigration was one that still functioned with mostly paperwork.

Ayuthaya introduced us to his friend, a young lieutenant, who began looking through files for Richard Shillander. It took him fifty minutes to cross-reference and locate all the forms recently completed by Richard when returning from out of the country.

On all the cards Richard had reported the same address, which we had already verified as a place where he did not live. I hoped that with the written cards as physical evidence and the investigator returning to state that Richard no longer lived at the residence, Ayuthaya could persuade his captain to initiate an investigation. Having spent years as a policeman, I appreciated the problem.

We gathered the cards, thanked the lieutenant, and went back to Ayuthaya's office to await the return of the other investigator.

Ayuthaya asked if we were hungry; it was past noon and obviously he wanted to eat. I wasn't hungry, but courtesy and common sense dictated that we not let this man out of our sight.

Ayuthaya directed us down a few alleys to his favorite lunch spot, a quaint restaurant where we bought food at a counter and ate outside under a large canopy. I generally don't eat at small, out-of-the-way Thai restaurants, but since Ayuthaya seemed to enjoy our company and the excitement of helping us, Scott and I decided not to decline and possibly offend our new friend. I ordered a dish with a lot of sticky rice, the mainstay of every Thai meal, and a barbequed chicken which was loaded with spices. Most Thai recipes start with a handful of hot chilis and get hotter with the addition of other fiery ingredients. Bangkok has many highly rated restaurants which reduce the hot spices for foreign palates, but this wasn't one of them.

After the short lunch we headed back to the Immigration building. The other investigator had returned to Ayuthaya's office and told us Richard and the children had moved four or five months previously.

"Yes," Ayuthaya agreed, "they have moved. But it was after Richard Shillander last returned to the country. He has not given us a wrong address."

"Isn't there a law," I asked, "saying a noncitizen must report a change of address?"

"Yes. But it is not enough for my captain to begin an investigation."

"Is there any other reason you could question Richard?" It was vital that Richard be kept occupied so Vivian could take custody of the children, or so we could hurry to the COG residence for the same purpose.

"No. I am sorry. I cannot question him without an investigation."

Ayuthaya excused himself to assist other investigators, who had just brought in a group of handcuffed illegal aliens. Most were from the Middle East and seemed to know each other.

The office suddenly buzzed with activity, and I feared we would get lost in the shuffle. Without Immigration's assistance, it would be difficult to recover the children short of a pitched battle.

"Ayuthaya," I said, when he returned briefly to his desk, "check one more document for me, please. I need to know when Richard last renewed his visa, and what address he used at the time."

"I can check with a friend in another office, but I am now busy with these prisoners. You can call me."

"Would you mind if I wait?"

"It is okay. You can wait here."

He placed a phone call. I could only pray it produced the last document I could think to check.

When Ayuthaya excused himself again, Scott leaned over and said, "Mike, we already know Richard reported the bad address on his reentry forms."

"Sure," I said, "but I never did hear if or when he renewed his own visa. He may have done it during the past few months. If he didn't, we'll need to come up with some alternative plan real quick."

"I think Ayuthaya wants to help, but his hands are tied."

"That's exactly right. We need to untie them."

Scott and I sat for an hour watching the commotion with the prisoners, and discussing the February 3 Europe trip. We were only a week away and had confirmed months ago with the company that we would be there.

We decided if Richard didn't show to renew the children's visas, he had most likely left the country. We would then have to travel to the villages on the borders of Laos and Cambodia and aggressively go after the COG houses, seeking information. By January 30, we had to leave with or without the children. Nothing else could be done after that point, and we would be wasting time and money if we stayed any longer.

"I have just called and they will tell me soon," Ayuthaya said.

"Is that your investigator identification?" Scott asked, pointing to a patch and picture pinned to his shirt.

"This is what you call a badge. It is our authority. Do you have any authority identification?"

"This is mine." Scott showed him our company badge and identification, an impressive-looking I.D. that could be mistaken for something more official.

Ayuthaya seemed impressed. Within a few minutes several investigators asked to look at and touch Scott's badge. I had assumed that law enforcement agencies around the world had some form of badge, but I learned many countries use a simple picture I.D. or a patch.

Ayuthaya brought over two more of his co-workers who were curious about the American private investigators.

"Ayuthaya," I said, meaning it as a joke, "Scott is a lieutenant."

Ayuthaya took me seriously. He introduced a sergeant and lieutenant, making certain to show them Lieutenant Biondo's badge.

"May I present my superior," Scott said to the two officers. "This is Captain Mike Intravia."

"Mike, forgive me," Ayuthaya said with a flabbergasted look on his face. "I did not know you were so important. It is a privilege to do you favor."

Ayuthaya finally introduced his captain, Hoontrakul, who apparently wanted to meet me because of my rank. The captain listened for a few minutes to my account of the plight of the Shillander children.

"I would be honored to help," he said.

"I'd really appreciate it," I said.

But what did "honored to help" mean? Ayuthaya

indicated we should leave Hoontrakul's office, and I found myself once again sitting with Scott amidst an atmosphere of total confusion.

Our luck, so far mostly bad, suddenly took a dramatic 180-degree turn. Ayuthaya's phone rang with the good news: Richard had renewed his visa a month ago, listing the address at which he *had not lived for several months*.

Ayuthaya immediately went back into Hoontrakul's office to see if he would authorize an investigation, and the captain gave him the go ahead. Ayuthaya told me, however, that he would be limited because he and his superior were both concerned about Colonel Thu Lee.

Of course. It was out in the open, and I should have understood earlier. Hoontrakul *could have* authorized Ayuthaya's cooperation based on Richard's not providing his change of address, but he hesitated out of fear of the brutal Thu Lee. I knew bone-deep he and all of us had plenty of reason to fear.

Ayuthaya accompanied us outside to see where we planned to park our surveillance vehicles the next morning and to point out the nearest bus stop. I figured Richard would come by public transportation.

Enterprising Alice Pifer waited on the plaza in front of Immigration to film Scott and me leaving the building.

"Smile," Scott said when he spotted the "20/20" personnel. "You're on candid camera."

Ayuthaya became very nervous. Instead of striking a Sherlockian pose, the Thai held his arm in front of his face and said to me, "No pictures. No pictures. I work undercover for the Immigration Department."

The cameraman complied when I asked him to stop. It was the first test of "20/20"'s cooperation, and I was happy to see he responded without question. Alice also agreed to completely block out Ayuthaya's face if they used the footage on the show. We then bowed, shook hands with Ayuthaya, and set a time and place to meet early the next morning.

Alice asked to film Scott and me walking in front of the Immigration offices on the street, and then interviewed us. The cameras drew an excited crowd of people trying to determine if we were American movie stars.

After the interview the inquisitive onlookers increased in number as they followed us down an alley to another street while the "20/20" cameras collected local color footage to be used as background for voice-overs in the television program.

Scott and I joked about our burgeoning movie careers, enjoying a short respite after the red tape entanglement with Immigration. But enough was enough, and I waved down a tuk tuk, a three-wheeled motorcycle that seats two passengers on the back, to return to the hotel.

As we climbed on board the rickety cab, a crowd became entranced by our being filmed. Alice was filming us from a short distance as we approached and entered the tuk tuk. Suddenly two motorists, turning to watch us instead of the road, collided. A motorcyclist hit the ground right in front of me, his bike bumping and skidding onto the sidewalk. The concerned crowd closed in to see if the bike rider had been seriously injured. Lying on the pavement, he grinned broadly, stood up and brushed himself off, apparently not hurt. Then he bowed, mounted his machine, and drove off waving to us.

Our audience, thinking him a stuntman in a planned comedy scene, laughed and applauded.

The driver then sped away, leaving the film crew on our way to the Ambassador where, having just arrived in Thailand, I needed to make travel arrangements to leave the country by January 31 at the latest.

Time passed quickly. At 6 P.M. Scott and I chose the Oriental Hotel to meet Vivian to go over plans for the next day. Alice had asked to film the meeting and interview us, and we found her waiting with the "20/20" crew.

"Vivian, Alice," I said. "Good evening."

"Did you have a good day?" Vivian asked.

"I believe so."

"That's wonderful. I hope all of your hard work and my prayers bring a happy result."

"Even if Richard doesn't show up, Vivian, our time hasn't been wasted. We'll have done the best we can."

I'd selected the Oriental Hotel believing it might lift Vivian's spirits. I had stayed previously in this splendorous hostelry during a protection detail that required my constant close presence to the business executive I guarded. His corporation spared no expense, in necessary contrast to the shoestring budget we gladly lost money on for Vivian and her chief sponsor, the First Baptist Church of Sioux Falls.

The Oriental may be the finest hotel in the world. That's how the television program "Lifestyles of the Rich and Famous" ranked it. The Oriental features 402 luxuriously appointed rooms, two magnificent swimming pools, a five-star-plus restaurant in the rooftop Normandie Grill, Lord Jim's Seafood restaurant, and the Authors' Lounge (the hotel was a favorite of Noel Coward and Somerset Maugham). Situated on the banks of the Chao Phraya River, the Oriental operates cruises on its own ships—the *Oriental Queen* and the *Orchid Queen*—and, depending on one's preference, tennis courts, squash courts, and a health center.

Everything about the Oriental is world-class, but it starts with unmatched service.

The meeting with Vivian and Alice lasted until 8 P.M. We discussed, over and over again, the details for Thursday: Vivian would wait in the van with Alice, and was instructed under no circumstances to leave unless directed by either Scott or myself; Alice and her crew would also wait for a signal from us before moving.

"Let's assume," I said, "Richard comes in without the children."

"All right," Vivian said.

"That is probably the greatest likelihood. Immigration will then question him, first getting his new address, which will be passed to us. Then we'll go there, pop in, and recover your children."

"Good. Wonderful."

"I want you ready to handle the children. No telling what they've been told over the years. It may not be easy listening to them, and it will hurt if they reject you. I want you prepared emotionally."

"I know."

"What if Richard shows up at Immigration with April and John, or he brings only Tito?" I had already determined what we should do, but I wanted her agreement. "Should we go with Immigration to the residence and try to recover all four at once, or take the ones he brings in and then hit the streets looking for the others? Hopefully, the children will cooperate, but that's hard to predict."

"I don't know what to do," she said.

"Why don't you think about it? We can talk tomorrow."

It was a hard decision for Vivian, but I knew what her answer would be. Taking the children Richard brought in and using them to help with the others was the only solution. We had successfully employed this strategy in Mexico.

Scott and I departed for the Ambassador, leaving Vivian and Alice to visit, but on the way we decided to detour to see the Thai boxing matches at Rajdamnern Arena. Thai boxing is to me the most exciting sport in the world. In Thailand it is part of their culture and each little town has its own champion.

The old Hollywood script in which a wronged American prizefighter says to his opponent, "Let's take the gloves off and duke it out like real men," could never be adapted to a movie about Thai boxers. Here the matches are brutal and raw. Unlike Western pugilists who wrap, tape, and lace their hands and feet in leather, Southeast Asians enter the ring barefoot, prepared to use elbows, knees, and body thrusts with jabs and kicks. Most professional fighters retire before they reach age twenty-five.

The packed stadium shook with sound, and the smell of liniment filled the air. The wintergreen odor mixed with the smell of thousands of people crammed into the arena to create a musky scent like nothing I have ever experienced. We gave a door attendant a 150-baht tip (a baht is about 3 cents) to find us a good seat, which turned out to be one row back of ringside. A bout had already started.

The fighters—most of them highly superstitious—wore charms, and little else, for protection. Music, on long drums and cymbals, played throughout the match, and even British soccer crowds seemed tame compared with this audience. Deafening best describes the sound, everyone standing, jumping, roaring—a mad cacophony.

I rationalized that it would have been a shame for two martial artists to travel halfway around the world and miss seeing these Thai boxing matches. As in a choreographed stage production, the aggression of the fighters increases in time with the musical arrangement. The music can have a controlling effect on the crowd—but not on this night. Instead the spectators became totally absorbed in the matches.

We might have been in a Las Vegas casino or on the floor of the New York Stock Exchange, so furious was the action around the crowd. It seemed everyone wanted to bet on his favorite fighter, and the money riding on the outcome drove the spectators to additional heights of frenzy. After a few bouts, we forced ourselves to leave and get some rest for the day upcoming.

Scott and I exited onto a dark street where taxis usually waited. However, the fights would not be over for a couple of hours, and cars had not yet lined up. We waited for a few minutes before realizing we would have to find a busy street to wave down a taxi. Neither of us knew our way around, so we walked in a direction we hoped led to a busy street.

It was very dark. A few Thais sat in front of storefronts visiting with friends, but there was nothing vaguely resembling a crowded, busy street. After a few minutes we found ourselves in a very rundown area.

With each car that approached, Scott and I walked into the street to wave down the vehicle, hoping it was a taxi. The few that passed us by already had passengers.

"This looks like trouble," I said, nodding at three men lounging against a building.

"You may be right. Let's cross to the other side. Maybe we can avoid them."

As we got closer, the Thais walked out into the street. A light from a sign that hung over a business gave us a good view of them. The three were dressed in loose-fitting, dark-colored pants with t-shirts and pullover shirts. Average size for Thai men, they exhibited a demeanor no different from a New York City mugger or a thug on a mean street in Buenos Aires.

"What now?" Scott asked.

"Say hello. Maybe we should introduce ourselves."

"They'll be thrilled."

"I don't think they have weapons. If they do, we give them everything they want."

"If they don't?"

"They get what they deserve." One of the trio pulled ahead of his friends and held out his hand, speaking a few words of broken English demanding baht.

Scott and I smiled, shook our heads, said we had no baht, and continued walking.

The other two positioned themselves to block our path down the sidewalk, while the first continued to demand baht.

I looked him in the eyes, removed the smile from my face, and said, "No baht."

There was no sense trying to sweet-talk our way out. They wanted either to take our money or have fun beating on us. I wasn't sure they didn't plan on doing both. Since we didn't consider ourselves outnumbered, there was no way we would give up money to three punks trying to scare us.

The one in the back lunged forward to attack, and the one in front put out his arm to stop him. He looked at me, smiled, and demanded baht.

"Can you believe this? A Thai Mutt-and-Jeff routine," Scott said, using a police phrase for one person playing the bad guy, aiming to frighten the individual into cooperating with the "nice" guy.

"It sure is. Let's stop this right away."

"Do it!"

Scott and I smiled at the Thais as we strolled forward. If they moved, we intended to walk by, continuing on our way.

But I knew better, and so did Scott.

When we were within a couple feet of the first Thai ("Jeff") he made a gesture to push me back. As he did, I blocked his arm and moved to his right side, then to his rear. I stepped around him and struck him with my elbow in his kidneys. He immediately buckled up, but I continued through, grabbing hair on the back of his head and pulling it back. I struck him with my right knee, then let him roll off onto the ground.

Just then one of the Thais kicked my left leg in the thigh with a boxing blow. The leg partially collapsed and I went to the sidewalk, but I rolled forward and back onto my feet.

Scott had been fighting with the Thai who had made the fake charge at us—Mutt. The one who had kicked me assumed a fighting stance, and appeared to have some Thai boxing experience.

Suddenly Scott put his attacker on the ground with a square punch on the chin. The felled man swung a slow, sleepy, awkward punch at my friend, who blocked it and stepped in with a strike to the nose and jaw. Scott locked his hands behind the attacker's head and pulled him forward, the face smashing straight into his knee. All the fight had drained out of this individual.

The remaining Thai froze and looked at me. I came out of my fighting stance. He pointed from me to Scott and yelled, "You die!"

Then he took off running down the street.

Now I was really concerned. We had to find a taxi before this character found a gun, or a bunch of his friends with machetes.

Scott complained about the blood on his pants as we walked at a quick pace up the street. We were both still tense and the adrenaline flowed strong but neither of us said much. Luckily, we had been heading toward a major intersection after all, and we quickly flagged down a taxi. It wasn't until I climbed into the cab that I realized how sore my left leg was from the kick.

We went immediately to the hotel to get a good night's sleep in preparation for a long day. I asked Scott not to tell anyone about the Thais trying to rob us. I knew the rather grubby incident, though unavoidable, brought us no honor, and it would simply create more concern for Vivian and possibly even Alice. I certainly didn't want it mentioned on the "20/20" show. It was something that happened to Scott and me, and was not part of the case.

13

Astonishment and Rage

JANUARY 28, 1988. Scott and I were up and ready to go at 5:30 A.M. We went for breakfast and I tried to eat, because I knew it would be a long day, but I wasn't hungry and my entire body felt rocky. Besides the sore leg, I identified the something else that had hit me because I'd experienced it before. I had apparently eaten some bad food at that lunch with Ayuthaya and suffered a touch of food poisoning. It wasn't bad and I could handle it, but it might make the day a little more miserable. Or maybe I wouldn't notice it at all. If we recovered the children on this critical day, more than a sore leg and food poisoning would be needed to dampen my good spirits.

Vallop sent an investigator to pick up Scott and me at the hotel. Vivian would be going with Alice in the ABC van.

I arrived at the Immigration building at 7:30 A.M. The day promised to be boiling hot, a brain-baker, a yearn-for-St.-Louis-in-mid-July scorcher. Already the temperature had risen into the high nineties, with humidity that made breathing difficult.

When the surveillance units and the van carrying Alice and Vivian arrived, I went from unit to unit passing out individual instructions. Everyone was nervous, wound tight as a piano wire, and each needed to be settled down. My own stomach churned, and not just from that bad food.

But how could anyone really be calm? This was D-day for Vivian and for all of us; it was now or never.

Kasame was one of the investigators Vallop sent. He drove the surveillance vehicle, but I derived some comfort knowing I would have direct control over him. Kasame's intentions were honorable but his ego dangerous. Still, he had sincerely attempted to prove his worthiness from the beginning, and maybe Vallop felt he had learned his lesson.

At 9 A.M. Ayuthaya was at his desk. We went over our plans again, and he walked me through the building, introducing me to some of the clerical people who might become involved.

At last I felt the bases were covered; now it depended on Richard. Had he fled the country? Had he decided to stay behind? We would know before the day ended.

I returned to the van where Vivian waited. I needed an answer to what she wanted to do if Richard arrived with only one or two of the children.

"Vivian, have you decided?"

"Tell me again what happens if he comes alone, or with only one or two."

"The Immigration people will demand that he furnish a correct address. They will pass this address on to us. Meanwhile, you take custody of whatever children he brought and go with me to recover the others. If he has provided a wrong address, we attempt to persuade your kids to help us. Of course, Immigration will be questioning Richard, and if we learn he has lied to them, and if the children won't cooperate, Ayuthaya will demand that Richard personally take him to the new residence."

"And what's the alternative?"

"Ayuthaya can order Richard to lead us to the house so the new address can be checked, and when we get there we can try to recover all the children at once. Or we can go there by ourselves. The thing is, if he brings some or all of your children to Immigration, we'll have the perfect chance to recover them legally. Ayuthaya will keep them separated from Richard during the questioning."

"I don't know what to do, Mike. I'm going to have to rely on you!"

"Let's recover any of the children that show up and use them to track down the others. If we wait to get them all at once—go to the house alone, or have Richard lead us there—it could be a wild goose chase, or other COG members might be alerted and spirit them out of our reach."

I returned to the Immigration offices and sat on a wooden

bench waiting for Richard. At 11 A.M., with no sign of him, I went down to the front of the building to check with Scott.

"What's happening?" I asked.

"A lot of hot air. Hundreds of people coming and going, but no sign of Richard or the children."

"The same upstairs. No air conditioning. But we've got a few less people."

"Kasame has stayed with his car, except to go upstairs once."

"I saw him," I said. "He talked to Ayuthaya."

"It's not looking good. I talked myself into believing Richard would come today."

"There's a lot of day left."

"You feeling any better?"

"No."

After checking on Alice and a coming-out-of-her-skin Vivian, I moved back inside the building. Lunch hour loomed just around the corner, a period when Immigration virtually shut down. The temperature inside and outside had soared to over a hundred degrees.

Lunch came and went, with minutes ticking by like hours. At 2:30 P.M. I was already planning the next day. I tried to remain optimistic, but the odds lengthened as daylight shortened. Even Vivian, Alice, and the crew had begun to despair.

I made my rounds of the van and the surveillance vehicles, prowling about impatiently, finding everyone exhausted, beads of sweat tracking down their foreheads, debilitated faces reddened by the draining heat.

The van featured air conditioning, but had to be turned off periodically to keep the engine from burning up. "What time does Immigration close?" Alice Pifer asked. I said 4:30 P.M., but we would wait until 5, in case Richard didn't know.

I figured Richard had been smart and made Thailand a memory after hearing about the Udon Thani fiasco. We had watched all day for anyone who might be a COG member checking out the Immigration office, possibly looking for us, but didn't spot anyone.

Returning upstairs, I sat down on the same hard wooden bench where I'd waited all day. Wringing wet, weakened by the enervating heat and recurring stomach cramps, I felt faint. I had to lean forward, prop my elbows against my thighs, and lower my head to keep from passing out.

The hallway hung quiet with day's end approaching. I checked my watch: 3 P.M., two more hours of torture to go. Then I heard the scrape, scrape, scrape of leather-bottom shoes on the marble stairs.

And there he was, *Richard Shillander*. There was no mistaking. A big man with a supercilious smile, his face had been etched as if by acid into my mind's eye through a hundred sleep-disrupting dreams.

He walked toward the visa renewal office, hardly glancing at me as I stared back down at the floor. He didn't even know the man who detested him and his cult.

I felt instantly rejuvenated—body charged, ready to go. It was good. If I couldn't get up for this challenge, what in life would ever move me?

Where were the children?

I had to take advantage of the opportunity presented. *He was right here*, this cause of seven months of nightmares for me—a lifetime for brave Vivian—and he needed to be handled just right.

"Ayuthaya," I said, pushing into the Immigration investigator's office, "are you going to question him now?"

"Not yet. But I know he is here. He must go down to the records, and then he will come to see me."

"Okay. You will get his address, won't you? And later, if need be, escort him to his house so you can verify the address?"

"I was told to tell him to come back in two weeks."

What? My heart sank.

"No. Don't do that. Please, Ayuthaya. Who told you to do this, my friend?"

"Vallop. He called me not so long ago."

"Listen, my friend. He was confused. Get Richard's address. If it becomes necessary, have him take you to the children, as we planned."

"Vallop said . . ."

"Ayuthaya, everything will be for nothing if you let Richard go. I urge you, do me this favor."

"I can do it, but I do not understand."

"Your favor is greatly appreciated, my friend."

I hurried downstairs to warn Scott about potential problems and to check on Kasame and the others. Scott stood at his post as I approached.

"Did Richard come alone?" The possibility existed that he had left the children outside with someone else.

"Yes. On the bus. No one with him."

"Is Kasame still in his car?"

"He was the last I looked. It's hard to tell, with all the vehicles parked next to his. I check every few minutes."

"I need to talk to Vivian," I said. "Have Kasame instruct the motorcycle surveillance unit to come around to the front lot. We may need it to follow Ayuthaya and report the COG house location."

"I'm on my way."

"Stay on your toes. We've already had some changes that almost repeated Udon Thani."

Excitement ran high in the van. Vivian shot off a dozen questions, one after the other, wanting to know what went on. I knew she had fought a hard battle with herself to keep from running after Richard and demanding he tell her where her children were.

After again making sure everyone understood her or his role—we intended to travel in the van to the address Ayuthaya provided—I took a moment to wonder why Vallop had changed my orders without telling me. Could he possibly have wanted to be the one who recovered the children at a later date, and thus become what he considered the "hero" of the operation?

I shook the thought out of my head. I truly believed it was merely confusion, perhaps a language problem, and Vallop remained the honorable man I knew him to be.

Now we played a waiting game. Alice coolly proceeded to make certain her own crew stood prepared. Vivian crouched tense, eyes riveted to the front of the Immigration building, where Ayuthaya would come out.

Scott approached the van, shaking his head, saying Kasame had disappeared and he had no idea where he might be. Scott wanted to look for the Thai, but I asked him to wait with us in the van. The next, and critical, events would occur soon.

Scott knelt near me, partially impeding Vivian's view. He muttered dark imprecations about the vanished Kasame, going nonstop . . . until the horror filled our eyes.

"Here comes Ayuthaya *and* Richard," Scott said, his voice a mixture of astonishment and rage.

"I don't believe it!" I sputtered.

"What's happening?" Vivian asked.

"Kasame's with them!"

What we watched was a disaster taking place right in front of our eyes. Scott and I took it in with a sort of numbed disbelief.

"What do you see?" Vivian asked, her voice frantic, our own shocked amazement transferred to her.

"They're getting into Kasame's car," I said.

"Tell me . . ."

There was nothing to tell her. Clearly Kasame intended to rescue the children himself, and if somehow he "succeeded," everything we had worked for was lost. *Vivian* needed to be present to take custody; otherwise it was kidnapping, and Thai police would be all over us, as we say in the United States, like white on rice. And if Kasame failed—that's the only thing he could do in this situation, fail—Richard for sure would flee the country.

"Scott," I said, "you remain with the van. Stand by and don't budge from this spot until you hear from me. Vivian, please do whatever Scott tells you. Alice, I need to take your other vehicle."

"Where are you going?"

"Wherever they go."

I exited the van as Kasame started up his vehicle. He intended to play chauffeur on his mad mission. Kasame, I realized, would never give up; he had to prove he could rescue the children.

I hoped at least that he would keep his mouth shut and not damage the case any more than he already had. Even this monstrous blunder might be overcome.

I opened the rear door of the ABC vehicle, surprising an interpreter and the driver with my sudden presence. They greeted me with amazed stares as I climbed into the rear seat.

"Good afternoon," I said. "I hope you're proficient at following people."

At least, I thought, *more proficient than I was at finding the right person to address.* I had aimed my greeting at the driver, who did not speak English.

"What's going on?" asked Narong, ABC's Thai interpreter.

"See that vehicle pulling out of the parking space? Follow it."

"But . . ."

"Alice said to do it."

"Is she coming along?"

"No. She'll meet us later."

"Let me talk to . . ."

"Hurry! They're leaving. Stay right behind them and talk with each other without staring at them. Whatever you do, don't lose them in traffic."

"Isn't one of them the guy we've been waiting for all day?"

"That's right. He's going to lead us straight to the children."

Narong translated my instructions to the driver, who lifted my spirits by peeling rubber getting from the parking lot into the street. But then, of course, he had to brake: We were immediately jammed up in heavy traffic. In all the world there couldn't be a worse place than Bangkok to try to follow someone.

I laid down on the back seat out of sight. If Richard figured out he was being tailed by a white man, he would know our intentions, and direct Ayuthaya and Kasame away from the children.

I also worried about Kasame looking back and seeing me. I didn't think he would purposely sabotage the investigation—his concern for Vivian's plight had been quite genuine—but his past record pointed to a man capable of committing more bungles.

Finally we crept out of gridlock, and from time to time I peered out at the car ahead of us. I had become increasingly comfortable with our driver, who had performed yeoman work in not losing our quarry in heavy traffic, and now we drove at the regular speed on an open road. We had been following for almost an hour and had traveled a good distance.

"Where are we?" I asked from my prone position on the back seat.

"Outside Bangkok. Maybe fifty miles."

"A direct route?"

"Yes. They have driven straight out of the city." The driver, apparently upset, said something in Thai.

"Richard has spotted us," Narong said.

"How do you know?" I asked.

"He keeps turning his head in this direction."

"Are you sure he's looking at us?"

"I think so."

"Tell the driver not to worry. Richard is probably looking at something else. Please inform the driver that I think he is doing a good job."

I had no idea whether we had been discovered. It really didn't matter, as far as what needed to be done. Most important, I knew Richard hadn't seen me. If he had spotted the two Thais, he likely thought they were Immigration agents.

Spotted or not, we didn't dare lose them. We had no choice but to continue the relatively close tail.

Our driver calmed down fifteen minutes later, when Richard, apparently at peace with himself, stopped looking back, and I carefully sneaked a peek out the window. Gone were the high-rise buildings of bustling Bangkok, replaced by occasional rickety shacks on stilts, and watery riceland. We could have been back in the tenth century, so undisturbed by time did everything seem.

Soon we bumped along through choking dust clouds that rolled through the windows, necessarily kept open because closing them led to a condition akin to suffocation. I wished for moisture, then wished I hadn't, as suddenly we found ourselves slogging along a mud path that seemed capable of swallowing both us and our vehicle.

Time moved slowly as I feared at any moment we would get stuck in the mud. I knew we were on the edge of a jungle, and couldn't resist taking a look. Outside stood a neat row of small wooden houses perched high on stilts along the bank of a canal. I saw sturdy farmers walking behind big oxen plowing fields, and peasants straining as they pulled carts through endless tracts of mud.

The houses had wooden-shuttered, glassless windows, open for light and ventilation. Large earthenware jars sat lined up on the ground to catch rain for drinking water.

Family members bathed and washed their clothes in the canal. These homes had no indoor plumbing, but each roof was equipped with an antenna to collect signals for any of them lucky enough to own a television set!

I wondered where we headed. If the Shillanders were living in a major COG commune, I faced serious and possibly dangerous problems. I had to get April, John, Caleb, and Tito away from Richard. But how? Robert Burke's advice flashed in my mind: *Find a way to have him give them to you,* so Vivian could take custody; otherwise we could expect a civil action which we couldn't win. Even Ayuthaya was powerless. He possessed no authority to force the father to release the children.

Burke had said I would find a way. Well, thus far it was eluding me. Maybe, I decided, I wasted effort bending my brain into a pretzel trying to develop a strategy before I knew what I was up against.

Some three hours into the trip we reached our destination: an isolated spot on the road too tiny even to be called a village. Kasame pulled off onto a dirt parking area in front of a compound featuring a worn sign that said "Red Cross," apparently an old relief agency center converted into apartments and housing for Thai locals and COG members.

Kasame drove through the entrance gate and out of sight. I instructed our driver to park and wait in front of a small abandoned store about fifty yards away.

My mind raced. *If* the children were in there, and *if* I could contact Ayuthaya, I might persuade the Immigration investigator to stall for three hours, *assuming* I could find a telephone to call Vivian.

Or maybe I could find a way to separate Richard from the children.

Perhaps I should let Ayuthaya leave, arrange somehow for Vivian to get out here, and then make the recovery effort. The problem with that was Richard would probably leave, kids in tow, before she could ever arrive. The compound's backyard was a jungle, and I suspected Richard knew how to escape into and out of it.

I didn't know how much help I could expect from Ayuthaya. I had pushed him to the limit, maybe beyond, in view of his having taken off with Kasame. I believed he would fear going any further, because of Colonel Thu Lee. I still hadn't determined Richard's relationship with the dreaded Lee, but if Richard called for help, and he responded, everyone might suffer—a deadly chance I couldn't imagine Ayuthaya being willing to take.

What to do? I wished I had a view inside the compound. If it contained a large COG contingent, the cult members would certainly ally themselves with Richard and pose a strong resistance to our small, paper-armed band.

I asked Narong to locate a phone, in case I needed to call instructions to Scott. We had planned our brains out, but ended up winging it.

Thirty minutes elapsed, but instead of Narong's appearance, Kasame's vehicle wheeled out of the compound. I strained my eyes to see.

The vehicle headed away from us, but skidded into a 180-degree turn and came back. Kasame was alone in the car. When he careened to a stop and got out, I already knew what he would say.

14

"Get Him to Give Them to You"

I HAVE NEWS," Kasame said.

I blocked an urge to strangle him. "I know," I said. "The children are here."

"How do you know?" He looked disappointed that he hadn't been able to surprise me. It hurt him, maybe more than if I had clutched his throat.

"Your poker face, Kasame. That gave it away."

"What do you mean?" He was smiling ear to ear.

"I'll explain later. Again you did something you were not supposed to. You must do exactly what I tell you from now on."

"I wanted to . . ."

"I know what you wanted. But your good intentions may cause us to lose the children. Were you in the military?"

"Yes."

"Then think of me as your superior officer. If we work as a team, we will bring the children to their mother. You must do what I say—nothing else, or more."

"I understand. I want to help."

"Good. I need your help now. Who does Richard think you are?"

"I did not tell him. He probably thinks I am Immigration, like Ayuthaya."

"How many people are there?"

"Richard. The four children. Richard's Thai wife. And a baby. That is all."

No army of cultists to fend off, I thought to myself happily. The new wife figured; I had theorized that something of this order had kept him in the country. Bigamy would not be considered an offense in Thailand.

"In what kind of residence do they live?"

"They have a house. It is away from the other apartments and houses, which are smaller."

"Will Ayuthaya come out to talk to me?"

"No. He is very worried. He says to tell you he has a problem. He loses his authority to remain in the house when the sun goes down."

Bad news. The sun was sinking quickly. and no way could Scott get Vivian here in time. We had an hour, maybe less.

I wandered away from Kasame, trying to concentrate. If Ayuthaya left, I knew he would forever wash his hands of the case and Richard would be ready to leave within minutes of his departure.

I had to take a chance—possibly our last—and it had to work. After many months of investigation, traveling halfway around the world—and knowing failure would gnaw at me for a lifetime—I determined I just could not go back without the children. My only hope was to confront the man I had tracked for more than half a year.

"Let's go," I said to Kasame. "I will follow you. Let me do the talking. Don't answer if someone asks who I am. Let me tell them." I turned to the driver, requesting him to remain with his vehicle until Narong came back. and then to join us inside. But just as I was opening the door to Kasame's vehicle, I spotted the interpreter trudging toward us down the road. He had indeed found a phone. All of us piled in with Kasame and he drove through the gate.

We traveled a small, snaking trail to the rear outskirts of the compound. The house where Richard, his new wife, and the children lived was small, shabby, windowless, with paint peeling from faded gray walls. But it was clean—COG houses are always clean.

I saw Caleb, Tito, John, and April playing near a muddy, stagnant pond next to the house. I had spent so much time looking at their pictures that I recognized them immediately.

I rapidly instructed Narong to go to a phone and tell

Vallop to send a runner to the Immigration parking lot and tell Scott Biondo to take Vivian to the Ambassador Hotel and wait there.

We had parked on the grass in front of the house. Exiting the vehicle, I pulled my badge case from my pocket, holding the documents from that South Dakota court in my other hand. It was a routine I had gone through many times as a police detective serving search warrants.

I wore sunglasses and an angry expression, which came naturally. For some reason sunglasses always distract and often aggravate people in a confrontational situation, so I use them to my advantage.

Ayuthaya stood in the kitchen talking with Richard and his common-law Thai wife, who held their infant son.

When Richard saw me come through the door, he turned quickly and strode toward me, clearly taking an offensive approach. This big man's eyes blazed like laser beams trying to melt me from his sight.

A part of me hoped he would do something foolish and provide the opportunity to release my anger. I thought of Moses David Berg and Flirty Fishing. But I forced myself to be professional and to control those feelings: uniting Vivian and her children was more important than unleashing my temper.

"I'm Agent Intravia with Allied Intelligence," I told him, "and I've come from the United States of America. Are you Richard Shillander?" I held up my impressive Allied Intelligence badge and identification for him to see.

"Yes, I am. What's this all about?"

"Two things: You filed false information with Thai Immigration, and I am here to serve these documents on you."

I opened each of the writs, one at a time, and read selected portions. When I recited the order giving Vivian custody, Richard stubbornly put his hands on his hips and his Thai wife exploded in a rage.

"Richard, what is this?" she shouted. "He cannot take children from you!"

Richard leered at her with fiery eyes. As a COG wife, she knew he was ordering her to shut up, which she did instantly, like a trained soldier.

Again his widened orbs seared my face.

"When you're in my house," he said, "take off those shades so I can see your eyes."

This was no fool. He tried to seize control of the situation, using his domain as a premise for telling me to take off the glasses. It resembled exactly being back on the streets of Berkeley. The sunglasses bothered criminals; good cops and street-smart people know eyes talk. But what made this petty debate over eyewear important was that it kept the conversation away from legal matters, on which I didn't have a leg to stand.

"Don't play games with me, Mr. Shillander. I'm not in the mood." I knew I had to play a hard, but cool-headed role. Unfortunately, the bestial hot house—all windows closed—did nothing to cool my temper.

"I don't like not being able to see your eyes," he said.

Good. Let's keep the debate on eyeglasses. "I don't care whether you like it or not. I'm not here to make you happy, or to be your friend. As a matter of fact, that's the last thing in this world I want."

"Take the baby in the other room," Richard snapped at his new wife. "And keep the children out of here."

"I want to listen," his wife replied, with surprising spunk. However, Richard's malign gaze sent her a clear message, and she sulked into another room.

"So what does this mean?" he asked me, in a tone designed to intimidate.

"It means Vivian has been given legal custody of the children by the courts of South Dakota. If you want to debate the decision, you can go to Sioux Falls and talk to the judge. For now, Vivian is going to take her children to their new home."

"This is typical," he sputtered, rotelike, "of the corrupt system existing in the United States."

His next action surprised me. "Get the children ready," he yelled to his Thai wife, "to travel to the United States with Vivian."

Get him to give them to you. He thinks he has no choice!

While Richard paced back and forth across the room, unconsciously scratching his head and studying the plank flooring, and his wife gathered the children's belongings, I inched over beside Ayuthaya. "Please," I whispered, "don't say anything to him."

Ayuthaya nodded his head slightly to let me know he understood.

Richard hadn't questioned my credentials or what authority Allied Intelligence had over his children. Nor had he bothered to ask if the South Dakota court order was valid in Thailand, or if he had to comply with it. He cooperated out of confusion. The official air with which I had presented the heavily stamped, sealed, and notarized documents in the presence of agents from Thai Immigration had stymied his progression of logical thought, and he assumed he had no choice other than to cooperate and comply voluntarily.

Keep everything moving, I told myself. *Don't slack up and give Richard time to question. Move it!*

Richard's woman walked through the room and called to the children from the front door.

April came into the house first, sensed something was wrong, and walked over to her father.

"You and your brothers must go with these men," Richard told her.

"Why?" she asked, recoiling and glancing over her shoulder at the solemn strangers suddenly thrust into her life.

The boys tumbled through the doorway, giggling, still wound up from a game of tag. Richard's words froze them in statuelike silence: "You are going to live with Vivian."

"No!" cried April, tears rolling down her cheeks. "I don't want to live with Vivian. She left us."

"The U.S. judicial system is controlled by the devil," Richard preached. "And this man has papers from his court. You all must go with them; we have no choice."

The Thai wife brought in two threadbare knapsacks, which had taken only ten minutes to pack with all their meager belongings, and dropped them by the door.

With all the children huddled around him as if for a locker-room pep talk, Richard said, "Keep in mind everything I have taught you over the past three and a half years. I warned you this day might come, so remember all the things I told you to do."

"We will remember, Father," they said in unison, following him down the front steps. I felt a chill run the length of my backbone.

"Where are you going?" I asked the Thai woman, who had crammed diapers and a baby blanket into a large straw shoulder-bag and slung the baby across her hip.

"I go with husband," she said defiantly. I would have preferred that Richard let us take the children to Vivian, but he and his wife demanded to go, and I had no authority to stop them. Once we got to Bangkok, Vivian could take custody, and it would be a civil issue between them for the courts to sort out.

I waited anxiously for Richard and the children to get into Kasame's vehicle, a twin-cab Isuzu pickup with a camper shell on the back.

Ayuthaya took me aside. "Mike, I hope you understand why I send Kasame to you out on road," he said. "I could not wait any longer. When sun goes down, I will lose my authority."

"You have been a good friend, Ayuthaya," I said, sincerely, not wanting to ask why he'd changed plans at the last moment. "We will now go to the Ambassador Hotel in Bangkok. Vivian will be there."

"I have no authority to make Richard take the children to Bangkok."

"Yes, I know. I don't either. But, as you see, he doesn't know we can't force him, so he has agreed to come with us and take the children to Vivian. Do you have the passports?"

"Yes."

"Can you give them to me?"

"No. I must give them only to the father or to the mother."

"Please, give them to Vivian."

"Yes. I will do this."

Ayuthaya had become extremely nervous. I had expected as much and considered myself lucky, almost the beneficiary of a miracle, that things had so far moved so smoothly. Ayuthaya again told me of his grave concerns about possible intervention by Colonel Thu Lee. I knew the Immigration investigator had more to fear from Thu Lee than any of us, since this was his home, but given the circumstances, the best result even for Ayuthaya was now a fast, clean, surgical removal of the children from his homeland. Out of the colonel's sight, out of his mind—I hoped.

I stood in the front yard wishing I possessed acting skills. Like a drill sergeant, I kept chest out, chin up, eyes front, attempting to portray an authority figure in complete charge. I wanted Richard's continuing cooperation stemming from the belief that he had no choice.

Richard placed the knapsacks in the rear of Kasame's truck. I stayed clear of him, knowing he would pry some more, needle me, probe for an advantage. No matter what, I couldn't misrepresent myself by orally proclaiming I was a government agent, or that the court orders he had been served with were legally enforceable in Thailand. I had to count on his own assumptions, and avoid conflict or questioning.

No chance of this. He strode toward me with a confidence I hadn't witnessed since shortly after my arrival. Somehow he had managed to screw up some courage, a development I feared would happen.

"Where is Vivian?"

I stared at the cultist with what I hoped was complete disdain. Actually, I felt revulsion. He had an unforgettable face: a sick, permanent smile plastered on his lips, intended, I suppose, to convey friendliness. But here was a man who never looked in a mirror. The smile twitched convulsively, rather weakly, actually, and didn't match the cold, cruel, exploiter eyes.

"Vivian was waiting for the children at the Immigration offices," I said carefully. "Now she is waiting to take custody of them at the Ambassador Hotel. She is with another agent from Allied Intelligence."

"Are you with the State Department?"

"No. I was assigned to track you down, to serve you with those official court documents, and to advise you to comply with what they order."

"It doesn't matter who you work for. You're from the United States and part of that corrupt, evil system the devil has taken over. My family left because of systemites like you. You carry the seed of the devil; he rules your every thought and action, and you and the other rotten systemites in America are too ignorant even to realize what has happened."

I wondered if he used this speech in recruiting seminars. I didn't doubt he meant it, though. The cloying smile stayed affixed to his lips, but the eyes that blazed were those of a fanatic. Unbidden, the picture of a book the COG sold flashed

into my mind: *My Little Fish*. It was one Moses Berg's sick
vehicles used to pass on his teaching to cult members.

"Look, pal," I said, "let me tell you who I am and what I
think. I'm the last person on the face of the earth you want to
mess with. I'm not here to listen to your song and dance about
the devil running the show in the United States; so be smart,
back off, and don't talk to me any more."

We engaged in a staring contest for a few moments, then he
turned, muttering "systemite," and walked away. I didn't like
what I felt. I prided myself on being a professional, but I was
furious and my violent side urged me to hurt this man.

COG had created a monster that exploited vulnerable
men, women, and children. I told myself it was COG, not this
product, that I really wanted to attack. If I had thought the
cult's influence could have been beaten out of him, it would
have been difficult to resist.

Richard seated himself and his children in the back of the
truck, and his wife and infant son sat with me in the back seat.
Kasame drove, with Ayuthaya next to him. The ABC "20/20"
vehicle followed, staying directly behind Kasame's pickup. I
knew it would take longer to return than it had taken to get
here, and not a moment would elapse without the danger of
something going terribly wrong—like Richard and the children
deciding to jump out of the bed of the truck and flee, an action
they had every legal right to take.

I constantly looked through the rear window of the cab.
Occasionally I caught a word, "devil," "evil," and "systemite"—
evidently they talked to each other that way—but never a full
sentence. Still, it didn't take a listening device or lip-reading
skills to know the subject of their conversation. Richard was
issuing last-minute instructions—surely on the subject of how to
escape, probably involving phone numbers they should call
to reveal their location, maybe safe-house addresses to which
they could run. The children, huddled around him, leaned forward in rapt attention.

There was nothing creative about this approach. The strategy is just as common in the United States. A parent, deprived
of visitation rights, often colludes with the children, hoping
they will collaborate in their own kidnapping. Of course, given

the circumstances—my powerlessness to stop Richard from just walking away with them—he employed a Rube Goldberg solution to his problem. It was also a potentially dangerous one. His "solution" might entail sending Thu Lee after the kids once he knew where they were being kept.

Richard's Thai wife questioned me, looking for leads that might help her husband. An attractive woman with long black hair, she apparently had been in COG long enough to learn the skills of manipulation. I noticed with her, as with the children earlier, that she regurgitated phrases like "pawn of the devil" and "corrupt systemites" that COG had drilled into her.

She tried numerous ploys to engage me in conversation. "You look like a nice man," she finally said. "I do not understand why you want to do this to Richard."

Give me a break, I thought. *Doesn't your mouth ever stop?*

I was tired, sick, and hoping for a quick, quiet trip back to Bangkok. I had to keep up my guard with Richard's wife. I was sure she had purposely sat next to me to try and obtain any information she could.

She continued to fire questions. I answered a few times with a look most people could easily understand, *Leave me alone.*

But she persisted.

"I don't think you want to hurt Richard," she said.

"Lady, please. Back off and be quiet. It's been a long day and I don't feel like talking."

"Why not?" she asked, her eyes full of anger, her voice shrill.

"Look, Lady," I bluffed. "I can drop you off on the road right here."

She sat silent for a few minutes, then tried her unusual brand of persuasion on Kasame. Leaning forward, touching his shoulder with her hand, she began, "You seem like a nice man. Why do . . ."

"Kasame!" I said, in my best schoolmarm tone. He turned and looked at me, and I shook my head. Kasame said something to her in Thai, and she glared at me, pulled the infant tight to her breast, and began mumbling words I assumed were a prayer.

Still Richard talked intensely with the children, and I saw on their part no slackening of attention. Even if we succeeded in transferring custody from the father to the mother, relaxation would be impossible until we were on a plane back to America.

The lights of Bangkok shone up ahead, blazing beautiful in the pitch dark. I told myself we had come too far for something to go wrong now, it simply would not happen. I wanted to wrap it up with no runs, no hits, no more errors.

But no telling what Richard had cooked up during his three-hour-plus powwow in the back of the truck.

15

"Do You Have the Passports?"

I EXITED THE ISUZU QUICKLY when we pulled up in front of the Ambassador lobby. Richard crawled from the back, as I held the rear door open.

"What would you do if I just took them and left right now?" Richard asked.

I answered him with an icy stare.

"I think I want the police here," he said, then turned to Ayuthaya. "No offense, sir, against Immigration."

"That's fine, Richard. You go call the police," I answered.

"Where's Vivian?"

"She'll be here in just a minute." I started to go get Vivian, who would be waiting with Scott upstairs, but Ayuthaya stopped me.

"If Richard starts to walk away," the Thai said, "I cannot stop him."

"I understand," I told him. If I could bring Vivian down quickly enough, it wouldn't matter.

I rushed into the lobby and dialed the room. The phone was busy. I ran to the elevator and luckily caught one that had just come down. Each second brought us closer to disaster. I galloped full stride down the hall, opened the door, and camera lights blinded me. Vivian, Scott, and the television crew were waiting in the room, expecting me to walk in with the children. They hit me with a barrage of questions, but I gripped Vivian's shoulders and said, "Hurry! The children are downstairs with Richard."

As we raced to the elevator, which I had put on hold, I tried to give her instructions.

"Quick!" she said. "Tell me what's happening!"

"Your children are okay. But Richard insisted on coming along with us."

"What is he . . ."

"It's a long story, Vivian. I want you to walk outside, take custody of your children, and get into the back of Kasame's pick-up. *Do not carry on any conversation with Richard*. You take care of your children, and we will take care of you."

"But . . ."

"Vivian! Say you understand!"

"Take custody of the children. Then get in the truck."

"Right."

"But what if Richard . . ."

"Don't worry about Richard. He's my problem."

Scott jumped into the elevator with us. I told him, "You're responsible for Vivian and the kids." Enough said. He knew exactly what to do. I could depend on Scott to remain calm, silent, and ready to respond instinctively. The doors glided open, we stepped into the lobby, and I led Vivian and Scott to the front of the hotel.

Vivian was excited and a bit confused, but as soon as we hit the door, she did exactly as I had instructed.

Scott moved quickly and smoothly at her side, watching the children and scanning faces of the hotel guests drawn to the source of the hubbub.

Richard darted over to intercept Vivian's beeline path toward the children. He had a sickly deceptive smile plastered on his face. It was a disarming, friendly facade he had learned to use well for the Children of God. Also, he had seen the cameras and his cult instinct to avoid trouble forced him to look pleasant.

The "20/20" news team had followed in an elevator right behind us and ran frantically with their equipment to capture the moment when Vivian took custody of the children. The presence of ABC was working beautifully as a diversion, exactly as I had hoped.

John, April, Caleb, and Tito were back in the truck, crying

and yelling, confused, scared, upset, their lives turned upside-down. They had no conception of who was right and who was wrong. All they knew was what they had been told by the cult and their dad over the years.

"How are you?" Vivian asked them.

"They don't even know you," Richard said. He stood towering above her, trying to intimidate.

"That's okay. They will."

"Who is this, you guys?" Richard asked.

"It's Mama," Vivian said quickly, "and I love you very much. Please don't worry."

"She's the one who left you," Richard said didactically.

"I'm your mother," Vivian said. Smiling warmly through watery eyes, she added, "I'm going to take you home with me."

Richard's baby-toting Thai wife elbowed her way into the family circle at the rear of the truck. "It's not right for you to go away with them," she said. "It is not right!"

The children, stunned by the questions and answers their parents hurled about, said nothing. Addled and unable to verbalize individually, they found strength in each other and began to reply in unison.

RICHARD: "Who do you guys love?"

CHILDREN: "Daddy!"

RICHARD: "Who is this, you guys?"

CHILDREN: "Vivian."

RICHARD: "Do we know her? Did she leave you years ago?"

CHILDREN: "Yes!"

THAI WIFE: "You kids do not worry."

RICHARD: "Who do you want to stay with?"

CHILDREN: "Daddy!"

RICHARD: "Come on out, guys. Come on. We're staying here."

VIVIAN: "No, you're not."

RICHARD: "They're staying here!"

VIVIAN: "The kids are coming to America."

Hearing Richard cue his children like Pavlovian lab subjects made me want to shut him up. Mundanely, I had been trying to find a driver. Kasame had vanished.

My search for a familiar face ended when I saw Vallop. He was standing in front of the hotel watching the tug of war between Vivian and Richard.

"Well, you're sure a sight for sore eyes," I said.

"I do not understand. Are you ill, my friend?"

"No, no. Forgive me. I should have said 'I am glad to see you.'"

"Ah yes. And I am glad to see that you have the children."

"I need to get them and Vivian out of here, away from Richard. I can't find Kasame. Do you have an agent who could drive us to the airport hotel?"

"Yes, two investigators are with me," Vallop said, pointing to the men standing together a few yards from us. "Which one do you like?"

"The man wearing the blue suit will be fine. Thank you for helping, my friend."

Vallop waved them over and gave instructions to the agent I had chosen.

My new wheelman walked to the driver's side of the truck, but when I turned away to talk with Alice Pifer, Blue Suit, like Kasame, disappeared.

The other agent walked over to the vehicle. I told him, "Airport hotel," and he acknowledged, sliding into the front of the truck as I went to the rear to help Vivian get inside.

Fuses burned short and I had to get my client and the children on the road before the whole scene exploded. Richard's saccharine smile for the cameras had transformed into a fount of aggressive verbiage. Backup troops—Kasame, Ayuthaya, and Blue Suit—had deserted and faded into the Bangkok background, not wanting any involvement once the commotion started. And I knew that police cars would soon be swarming on the Ambassador parking lot to investigate a reported disturbance.

We had done nothing illegal, but we would all end up at the police station, with Scott and me sitting in a cell for a few days trying to explain that it was a civil matter between Richard and Vivian.

As I hurried to the back of the vehicle, I found Vivian still standing outside, arguing with Richard over the papers.

"Scott!" I yelled. "Get Vivian into the truck! We're leaving!"

Madness had set in. The bickering continued.

"Vivian," I said, "I've already served him. It's time to go."

Richard lunged toward Vivian, and I stepped between them, pushing him away with an open hand against his chest. Scott helped Vivian into the rear of the pickup with the children.

I moved back to the front of the vehicle to get into the passenger seat. I heard young, confused voices crying, and older ones quarreling.

The children spouted abusive jabs at Vivian, denouncing her as someone who had abandoned them. She urged them to pray with her, but one of the boys countered loudly, "You're the worst mommy in the whole world!"

Vivian pleaded tearfully, exhorted them to give her a chance. But they turned cold shoulders and hurtful words on the woman who Daddy said had "run away and no longer cares."

I started to climb into the front seat—and discovered our second driver had also forsaken us. All of the Thais were gone. With the yelling, pushing, and confusion, they had reacted by walking away from the problem.

Worse, Richard had opened the door to the rear seat on the driver's side, apparently intending to travel to the Airport Hotel with us.

My flying-by-the-seat-of-my-pants plans were rapidly falling apart. Deciding to drive the vehicle myself, I ran around to the other side.

Richard was halfway in by the time I reached him. I grabbed the back of his shirt and belt for leverage, yanked him out, and spun him away from the truck.

Then I became aware of a wonderful sight: Suddenly standing by my side to help was Kasame!

The man who had caused so much grief had returned at the critical moment, after everyone else had jumped ship.

"What do you want me to do?" Kasame asked.

"Will you drive us?"

"Yes."

He hopped behind the wheel and started the engine.

Richard, like a boomerang, was back, trying to enter the rear seat again. I stepped between him and the vehicle, locked the door, and shut it. He moved forward, and I struck him on the chest with an open hand to prevent him from coming any closer.

"You're not going with us," I said.

"Why not, why not?" cried his Thai wife.

We stood staring at each other, Richard and I, a moment frozen forever in my memory. Then he dropped his eyes. We both knew it was over. He still had that sick grin on his face when I told Kasame to drive away, and I ran to catch up with the vehicle, jumping into the front seat while it moved across the parking lot. I turned to see if Richard would take a taxi to follow us, but lost sight of him among all the people who had gathered.

"Kasame," I said, "don't get on the expressway yet. Stay on the streets so I can check to see if we're being followed."

Skilled at losing tails, he wound us through an intricate maze of back streets and alleys. After ten minutes of twists, turns, and backtracking, we agreed that the coast was clear and headed north.

As we clipped along at a steady pace on the Bagna-Port Expressway, I looked at our passengers in the back of the truck. Scott sat patient and alert, and Vivian desperately tried to explain to her children what had happened. They shook their heads defiantly.

We had a plane to catch just after midnight, and I had rented a room at the hotel to use as a hideout until flight time. Confident that the airport would be crawling with Richard and all the COG members he could round up on the spur of the moment, I planned to hole up at the hotel with Vivian, the children, and Scott. He or I would go in advance to the terminal to scout out possible trouble.

We arrived at the hotel with not a lot of time left before our flight. Figuring that the children were famished and that eating would keep them occupied while I made final preparations, I opened the back of the truck and said, "We're going to stay here for just awhile before we leave for the airport. Who's hungry?"

Caleb said, "I am. We haven't eaten all day."

"What can we eat?" Tito asked.

"What would you like?" I said.

"Some fruit."

"Do they have ice cream?" April asked.

"I'm sure they do. Let's go to the room and you can order whatever you want from room service."

"Don't listen to him," said John, the oldest. "He wants to spoil you. That's exactly how the devil plants his seed. He spoils you, then takes advantage." His face wrinkled into an impudent pout as he spat words at me: "I bet you spoil your children, and evil is planted in them. They probably have no respect for adults."

"You know what, John? You're right," I said calmly. "Sometimes I do spoil my children, out of love. But even though I spoil them, my two daughters have never shown me the disrespect you have been showing your mother."

While John's protest waned and he waxed silent, searching for an appropriate response to make as the newly self-ordained, pants-wearing head of the family in his father's absence, I took Vivian aside.

"How are you holding up?"

"It's tougher than I thought. I just thank the Lord for bringing them back to me."

"We have to make sure we keep them. I saw Richard plotting with them and am sure they have a plan to get away from us."

"They're completely under his influence right now. I know that will change when we get them to a different environment."

"Keep them away from phones. Don't let them wander out of your sight."

"I won't. Believe me, I won't."

"Did the Thai Immigration man give you the passports?"

"No."

"Scott!" I yelled. "Do you have the passports?"

"No. Ayuthaya left the minute we came out the lobby of the Ambassador."

This presented a gigantic problem. We had the children and plane reservations, but no passports. Ayuthaya was obligated to give them to one of the parents, and I feared, in the confusion, he had handed them to Richard.

"Okay," I said. "Go inside to your room. I'll take care of it."
But I didn't know how.

"What does this mean?" Vivian asked.

"It means we're stuck here until we can obtain new passports."

"Can we get them in time to catch that flight?"

"No."

"How about the Friday flight?"

"I don't know. We'll need help from both the U.S. Embassy and Thai Immigration, and we'll need it fast. Immigration is closed on Saturday. Don't worry yourself with it. Just take care of the children. You have your work cut out for you."

"God bless you and Scott."

"I hope He does, Vivian."

16

Riding the Red-Tape
Merry-go-round

WE HAD CHECKED INTO TWO ADJACENT ROOMS, with Vivian
and the children in one, Scott and me in the other.
Kasame stayed to help. On the ride up the expressway, he had
complimented the way I worked, likening it to his own modus
operandi.

I positioned Kasame in the hallway to prevent any of the
children from escaping, and Scott returned to the Ambassador
to pick up our luggage and check out. By the time I had everyone situated and myself on the phone, it was early Friday morning with little hope of finding anyone who could pull enough
strings for us to exit the country during the weekend.

I asked the Marine sergeant on duty at the U.S. Embassy to
please have Ed Wehrli return my call as soon as possible. I had
two immediate objectives: getting new passports for the children, and protecting them from COG, which surely wanted
back what it considered "valuable assets."

Peripheral worries included Richard telling the police
we had kidnapped the children, and the law, unaware of what
really happened, coming after us. Or, more onerous, Richard
might put a "sic 'em" bug in Thu Lee's ear.

I called St. Louis and told the office what had occurred.
Then I phoned Patti and said, "We have the children."

"Thank God. When are you coming home?"

"We've run up on a passport snag, but I hope we'll be out
of here tomorrow."

"Are you in danger?"

"No more than expected. Please don't worry, honey. We'll be home in a few days."

"You wouldn't tell me if you were knee-deep in sharks. I know that, Mike. But please take care."

"I love you. Give the girls a hug from me."

"I love you too. Be careful, and bring those children home."

Talking to Patti relaxed me. It had been a long, hard day, and I still had plenty to do before we could leave Thailand.

The phone rang. It was the embassy. The individual on night duty had been given my message, and I explained who I was and that I had been communicating with Ed Wehrli. I pleaded for assistance in obtaining passports for the children, so we could leave on the Friday flight, but he stayed with procedures, telling me to come in when they opened at 7:30 A.M.

"This is an emergency. I have a mother and four children who are in danger."

"They'll be safe at the embassy."

"I'm worried about *before* we get to the embassy."

"We open at 7:30."

"I'd like you to make an exception here."

"That would be difficult to arrange. I'd have to . . ."

I gave up beating my head against this bureaucratic brick wall.

But I couldn't give up. We had to get out of the country quickly. The longer we stayed, the greater the danger. I called Brad Beckstrom to have the church begin preparing for the Shillanders' return.

"Mike, good to hear from you," Beckstrom said. "Everyone here is on pins and needles. We've been holding prayer vigils, asking God to give you the strength to find the children for Vivian and bring them home safely. Is the news good?"

"Yes and no. We found all four children. They're with Vivian, and everyone is safe."

"Thank God for that. What did you mean, 'yes and no'?"

"We don't have passports for the children and need to have new ones issued. I spoke with the embassy and was told to come in tomorrow. Is there any chance that you and Senator Pressler could exert some influence to open the embassy doors for us tonight? We could spend a half-day on passports, and we need that time to get through Immigration."

"I'll get in touch with the senator immediately."

"We really should get out of here as soon as we can."

"I know what you're saying, Mike. I'll get right on it."

That was that, unless Beckstrom and Pressler came through for us. I walked into the hallway and found Kasame alertly standing guard. I knocked at Vivian's door and she came out and spoke with me. Some local church people had come over to help with the children, and visit for a while.

"Vivian," I said, "we'll spend the night here. I can't find out anything about new passports until the embassy opens in the morning. So you and the kids try to get some sleep."

"Okay. My friends will stay for another hour, then it's lights out. We're all pooped. These are good people and their being here has helped a lot. Christian fellowship is a powerful thing; the children have settled down. It's going to be hard for them to adjust to the change."

Alice and her cameraman had arrived at the hotel. They asked Vivian for an interview with the children, but only when she felt comfortable they could handle it. Alice stayed true to her word, always remaining very conscious about the welfare of the young Shillanders.

The food poisoning and fatigue caught up with me. Feverish beads of sweat soaked my forehead and I felt like a knife turned in my gut. I called room service for aspirin; we had a long way to go and I had no time to be sick.

Scott returned with our luggage. He also looked exhausted, but refused to admit he was running out of steam.

"When are we getting out of here?" he asked, then did a double take. "Mike, you're white as a ghost!"

"Food poisoning. I'll be all right. How are you doing?"

"This has been the longest day of my life."

"Where and how did you finally get those kids?"

"Richard had them in a shack out on the edge of a jungle at a big commune-type compound."

"Nice place, huh? Sounds like hell."

"Just as hot; the windows were shuttered tight as a drum."

"I hate to keep asking, but when *are* we getting out of here?"

"I put a call into the embassy and was told to come at 7:30 for passports. I also talked with Beckstrom, who is going to see if Pressler can help us get the doors opened before then."

The phone rang. It was Ed Wehrli calling from his home. The State Department had contacted him, requesting special consideration be given to expedite passport applications for the children. Senator Pressler and Brad had come through with flying colors.

Wehrli agreed to drive to the hotel immediately with applications and personally help us complete them for prompt processing first thing in the morning.

I phoned Brad and thanked him for his help. He told me to call back if I needed anything else.

Ed Wehrli was knocking on my door at about 1:30 A.M. He seemed not in the least put off by the hour but rather pleased he could help. He congratulated me on getting this far.

I contacted Vivian in the other room and she joined us with all the vital statistics for the forms.

After all the blanks were filled in, Wehrli perused the papers one more time. "Well," he said, "I think this will fly after we attach individual pictures of the children."

"Is there a passport photo shop nearby?" I asked.

"Sure. They're all over the city. But I don't know of one open at two in the morning."

"Vivian, do you still have your pictures of the children?"

"Yes, in my room. I'll get them." She tiptoed next door and brought back a packet of snapshots. The three of us examined the pictures, but they were tattered and faded from months of handling.

"I doubt Immigration will accept these," Wehrli said, shaking his head. "They're quite picky about clear, sharp, and more importantly, recent photo identification."

"Okay," I said, "let's make new ones. I have a Polaroid in my suitcase." But when I went for it, I discovered my luggage had been forced open and both a 35mm camera and the Polaroid were missing. *Great!* I thought, *what else can possibly go wrong?*

Vivian wilted with disappointment, and I racked my fever-heated brain for a solution. Finally I said, "Well, we'll just have to make do with what we have and cross our fingers that Immigration won't beef." I culled out the four best pictures and, using a pair of manicure scissors from Vivian's makeup bag, trimmed them down to regulation size.

When I asked Wehrli if he would accept them, he said, "Yes, but Thai or U.S. Immigration may not."

"I'm willing to take a chance with the Thais," I said. "And if we make it to American soil, Immigration will have to accept us, like it or not, what else can they do?"

Wehrli acknowledged my point and left with applications and pictures to be processed at the embassy. He told us to be there at 10 A.M.; he would have them completed by then.

At 3:30 A.M., Vivian and the children slept, but Scott and I were wide awake, and Kasame remained in the hallway. We kept our door open to make regular checks in the hall. With each noise, Scott jumped to his feet and looked out. Each time he found Kasame on watchful duty.

I put in an overseas call to Teri Schuchman, who had been changing our travel arrangements continuously throughout the trip. Teri made reservations for us to fly out at 5:30 P.M. Friday afternoon, which would give us plenty of time to clear Thai Immigration. Scott and I had tickets that could be traded for new ones when we arrived at the gate, and I assumed Vivian and the children had the same kind.

Everyone remained on standby at our St. Louis office. A backup team stood ready to take the next flight out if I needed them.

After ordering up breakfast at 7 A.M., Scott and I prepared to move everyone. We intended to start the day with a trip to the embassy first on the agenda.

I was concerned that Richard or the COG might either be in the embassy, or watching it closely. I assumed Ayuthaya had given the children's passports to Richard, who would deduce that we would head there to get replacements.

We packed our luggage and checked out of the hotel. Alice agreed to take Vivian and the children in her van, which would allow her to do some interviewing in transit. Scott went in the van, and I rode with Kasame.

When I arrived at the embassy shortly before 10, Scott made a sweep of the place. He found no sign of Richard or the COG, so I quickly entered and went to Wehrli's office.

He handed me the passports and said, "By the way, Richard Shillander came in early this morning to file a complaint."

"I'm not surprised," I said. "He may be lurking out in the bushes and try to grab the kids. What happened with his complaint?"

"He was told nothing could be done. I hope you've seen the last of that character. Good luck, Mike," he said, shaking my hand.

Scott went with Vivian and Kasame to Immigration to have the passports stamped, while Alice and I stayed with the children in the ABC van in a remote Bangkok parking lot. From there I planned to head straight to the airport when I received word from Scott.

Scott maintained an eagle eye at Immigration. Richard had been to the embassy and would most likely also voice a protest at Immigration, where he had a better chance of success. I hoped Scott could get in and out of there in a matter of minutes.

It didn't happen. When officials checked the records, they found documentation showing that only two of the children had entered the country. Kasame and Scott pleaded with Ayuthaya (who in the confusion had indeed handed the passports to Richard), but they met an unyielding wall of resistance. Because of a major influx of illegal aliens, Thailand had adopted strict regulations for entrance and exit certification, and Ayuthaya was powerless to bend the rules.

We sat on the parking lot for hours, moving a few times with the sun to take advantage of shade trees. The children were well behaved for the most part, and actually became enjoyable to be around. John and April, being the oldest, were the most confused. I knew all of them hurt a great deal inside, and from time to time it showed.

Frustration mounted throughout the day as the wait stretched to almost eight hours. Cars would pull onto the lot and I peered at each one eagerly, hoping to see Scott and Vivian so we could be on our way.

Alice and the crew were as anxious as I; they had become

emotionally involved in the case, adopted it as their own, just as the people in South Dakota had.

At 6 P.M., a half-hour after our plane left, Scott, Vivian, and Kasame returned with the bad news.

"After you got the passports from Wehrli," Scott explained, "things went steadily downhill. Clerks pawed through files all day but couldn't find entry papers for Tito or Caleb. As far as they're concerned, since only two Shillander children entered the country, the other two don't exist so they can't be processed out. It was a real bummer."

"Yes," said Kasame, "We could not make any . . . how do you say? . . . headway with the officials. They would not change policy for us."

Scott added, "I even offered to bring an Immigration inspector out here and show him the children—one, two, *three*, *four*—but that didn't work either. So we have to hang around for two days before getting back on the red tape merry-go-round Monday morning."

"What do we do now, Mike?" Vivian asked.

"When you didn't show up in time for us to make it to the airport," I said, "I began asking myself the same question. We need a safe place for you and the children to stay—one that's off the beaten path where Richard wouldn't look for them. I think the Baptist Guest House is our best bet."

"I agree," she said. "The managers know me and my situation."

"Okay," said Scott, bringing his hands together in two loud claps to amuse the tired children, "let's head 'em up and move 'em out. Wagons hooooooo!"

I felt we would be safe at the Baptist Guest House for the weekend. The American couple running the inexpensive hotel established for Christian visitors and missionaries were friends of Sioux Falls church members, and I could trust them. Plus the building and grounds offered good security, completely enclosed by a wall topped with barbed wire and broken glass to prevent anyone from climbing in.

We arrived there at 7 to an open-arms acceptance. While we settled in quickly, Alice and her crew returned to their hotel and Kasame went home for the night. The Guest House staff whipped up a late dinner for us and Scott joined Vivian and the children in the dining room. I still ached from the food poisoning, and the thought of eating made it worse.

I got on the phone again, calling Brad, my office, and Patti. They were as disappointed as we were, and concerned for our safety.

Scott and I constantly worried that the children might attempt to escape, or to contact their father so he could snatch them. All four—especially John and April—would bear close watching.

I was numb and needed rest. Our room had a ceiling fan that hummed as it turned, and on the wall between our beds hung a picture of a Thai farmer standing under his basket-weave hat in the middle of a field.

My bed was small and hard. I closed my eyes, hoping to fall into a deep sleep, but my mind still raced in high gear, recalling recent events and conjecturing over troubles that could happen while we remained locked in Thailand. We had to survive at least two days before we could possibly resolve the problem on Monday and flee the country.

My eyes were wide open, though I fought desperately to keep them shut and let everything go for a short while. Scott, also near exhaustion, had gone out onto the grounds to pull three hours of guard duty.

I got up, dug into my luggage, found my Walkman and training tape, plugged in the earphones, and placed the tape-player in the pocket of my sweat pants.

"Highway to the Danger Zone" filled my head, and the body that a few minutes ago had collapsed like a cadaver on the bed came alive, strong and ready for motion. The music put me into something resembling a trance, and I began doing what is called forms, a series of blocks, punches, and kicks meant to simulate a fighting situation.

It was invigorating to let everything out, holding back nothing. After the steady, pulsating rhythm drove my workout through four songs, I felt the tension wash from my body and brain. I sat on the hard floor with sweat dripping off me in the dark of the night, rested, and listened to "Eye of the Tiger" from *Rocky III*.

Eyes closed, legs crossed, back straight in a traditional

karate position, I listened carefully to each word and played it again. When the song ended and I pulled out the ear plugs, I was jarred by the sudden silence and peace of the room where I would now be able to slip into the arms of sweet Morpheus, if only for an hour or so.

I knew the answer to bringing the children home: Keep the will to succeed and survive.

▲ April, Caleb & Tito playing at the Guest House.

◀ Caleb, Tito, April & Camera Crew waiting on parking lot while Scott and Vivian were at the immigration office.

17

Soldiers in the Courtyard

SATURDAY, JANUARY 30, 1988. Our rooms on the second floor overlooked an emerald green courtyard with chairs, benches, and a small playground near the main gate. Scott and I joined Vivian and the children for breakfast in the main building where hotel guests dined together boardinghouse style.

The children were in good spirits, and seemed to be warming to Vivian. John, quiet and still, kept his distance, but Caleb and Tito enjoyed themselves, excited about the excellent breakfast they ate. April had become more talkative, firing off a steady stream of questions. A very smart young lady, I suspected, she would be the one who would try to reach her father.

After breakfast the children returned to their room briefly, then came out with Vivian to play. Scott and I were on the grounds watching for trouble from outside and within.

The day went well, with Vivian and the children growing closer together and becoming a family again. Scott and I enjoyed watching the boys try to outdo each other with skin-the-cat and balancing acts on the swingset. Once, when April thought we were totally engrossed in her brothers' performance, she slowly worked her way to the gate and we had to caution her to stay back.

Later in the day I overheard April at the reception desk asking the manager, "Could you give me a brochure, please?"

"No," he said, "we don't have any, but here are some postcards if you're interested in a picture of the place."

165

It hit me what she was doing: looking for an address. As I approached her, April glanced up and knew I was on to her little scheme. She let the cards slip from her fingers and walked away before I could say anything.

I asked the couple in charge not to allow the children to make calls from the lobby telephone. I suspected April already had the address, or at least the name of the Baptist Guest House and would now look for a way to get the word out. Luckily, there weren't many people in the hotel from whom she could solicit help. Besides, unless it was another child, the guests at the hotel would not likely assist her. Rather, they would come to us.

Evening came and Vivian and the children settled into their room. The hotel manager, helpful in a tense situation, drove to a video store and returned with movies for the Shillanders to watch.

Scott and I alternated shifts throughout the night, keeping a worried watch over the compound.

Sunday, January 31, 1988. Sunny and hot. The courtyard where Vivian played with her children featured lush green grass, tropical plants, and a bright rainbow of blooming flowers surrounding the inside of the wall.

I stayed busy on the phone, trying to pull strings to facilitate our exit from the country. Each hour that passed increased the risk. I knew it was only a matter of time before Richard, or COG, or worse—Thu Lee—made an unwelcome appearance. I called Brad Beckstrom.

"Mike," he said, concern edging his voice. "You wouldn't believe the number of calls we've been receiving. What's going on?"

"We're doing everything possible, but we're caught up in red tape. Immigration has lost two of the children's entrance cards. They won't affix exit stamps on the new passports until it can be shown they *entered* the country. A Catch-22. Even though they're here and have passports, they have to prove they got here. Is there anything you can do to help?"

"I'm not sure. I'll talk with Senator Pressler again. He's as anxious as everyone else. If you call back a little later, I'll let you know what ideas he has."

"Another favor, please. I need you to clear the road with

Immigration in the United States. I used family pictures for the passports, and I'm afraid we may get caught in more red tape when we arrive."

I didn't add, *if* we arrive.

"I'll mention it to Pressler, but I'm not sure what he can do. I do know he very much wants to see you bring the children back. Call me in an hour. And good luck."

I called Vallop and asked if he would visit Ayuthaya and anyone else he might know to use his influence to inspire the bureaucracy to action. He said he would do his best.

I contacted the embassy and left a message for Ed Wehrli. He phoned back fifteen minutes later.

"Thought you would be out of the country by now," he said.

"We ran into bad luck. Thai Immigration lost two of the children's entrance cards. They won't give us exit stamps until they find the entrance documents. Is there anything you can do?"

"It seems picayune—obviously, they can see the children are in the country—but Thailand has very strict rules regarding immigration, and sound reasons for maintaining them. The problem arises when there are justified exceptions to the regulations."

"I'm worried about the safety of Vivian and the children."

"That's what I mean about a justified exception. But you need to understand, the Thais are very regimented, and the people you're dealing with aren't likely to make a decision on their own. Let me try to reach someone higher up who has the authority to handle this situation."

"I'd appreciate it."

"It's my pleasure. We were delighted to see you pull those children away from that cult."

"Brad Beckstrom, Senator Pressler's aide, is trying to help from his end."

For a moment I thought the line had gone dead.

"Please don't do that, Mike. Let us handle this for you. I believe it will be a formality after I make my phone call. It does not look good, politically, if a U.S. senator is summoned to resolve something like this. I'm afraid our relationship with Thailand could be damaged."

"I'll do what I can. But if Pressler can help, I can't in good conscience turn him down."

"I appreciate what you're saying, but the senator's intervention won't be necessary. I'm sure we can resolve this, and you'll be on your way tomorrow morning."

Wehrli's words encouraged me. Certainly his embassy clout should make the difference. I had already learned that in Thailand it's who you know that gets the job done.

I called Teri Schuchman.

"Mike, are you okay? Everyone is worried."

"We're fine; just spinning our wheels. There's a good chance we can leave tomorrow. What can you get for us?"

I waited while she punched a few computer keys.

"I have you on Thai Air, Flight 606, departing Monday, February 1, at 3:45 P.M., with stops in Hong Kong and San Francisco. I hope that will work."

"Perfectly, I think. What about Vivian and the children?"

"Do they have tickets?"

"I'm sure they do."

"There will be plenty of room on the flight. They can exchange their tickets at the airport."

I phoned Patti and my office with the itinerary update. Putting down the receiver, I heard shouts outside: "Let me down! Leave us alone!"

I rushed out into the courtyard and saw Scott returning from the gate carrying Tito and April like two sacks of potatoes slung over his shoulders.

"Put me down!" Tito screamed while his feet kicked the air in front of Scott. "You can't do this to us!"

John and Caleb stood sullenly in the courtyard staring at the man who had aborted the escape attempt of their siblings. We led all four up to Vivian's room. With faces filled with confusion, they yelled at us saying they would not return to the United States. We vowed to exercise much stricter control.

"They were fast," Scott said, when we were alone in the hallway. "I almost didn't catch April."

"We need to keep them locked down," I said, unhappy with the new role of jailor.

"I agree. Allowing them to play in the courtyard is too risky. What if all four had run in different directions?"

Wehrli called and said the head man at Immigration had debarked for one of Thailand's border provinces and wasn't expected back for *a week*.

"How bad is this news?" I asked.

"We don't have any problems, Mike. I'm sure his office can reach him in the morning. I'll draft a letter to him—his name is Commander Wanich Kullama—from the American embassy, and we will cut the tape."

I hoped so. But I nonetheless called Brad Beckstrom.

"I spoke with Senator Pressler," Brad said, "and he thinks the way can be cleared through U.S. Immigration. He'll contact the State Department, which should be able to help. The red tape is a different story. The senator said he'll call the Thai ambassador, but he doesn't know if it will do any good."

"I appreciate whatever help he can give. I've been told by Ed Wehrli that the immigration problem will be taken care of first thing tomorrow morning."

"He's probably right. The embassy has good relations with Immigration."

"Still, I'd like to have another loaded gun."

"I understand."

"If you haven't heard from me by noon Thai time, would you call the Thai ambassador? I know it will be late at night your time, but even that could work in our favor by stressing the urgency to the ambassador."

"Okay. This is all new to us. All we can do is what we hope will work."

At least the way had been cleared if we did reach American soil. The big problem, as it had been since the beginning, was getting there alive, and with the children.

Scott and I made plans for the next twenty-four hours. We decided that Monday morning he would remain behind with the children in their room at the Guest House, and I would go with Vivian and Wehrli to Immigration. I hoped to return by 10:30 A.M., and leave at 11 for the airport. I did not want to risk getting caught in a traffic jam and missing the plane, or having inadequate time for preboarding preparations. If things went according to schedule, we would arrive several hours early, clear customs, and be the first people on that airplane.

Before she settled down for the evening, I asked Vivian to pack her bags, everything except clothing for the next day.

Scott and I figured on a long night. I stood the first guard shift and Scott relieved me. About 2 A.M. I went to the courtyard to take his place.

That's when the gun-toting soldiers arrived, and I didn't doubt they were Thu Lee's men. We played a silent cat-and-mouse (we were the mice) game with them, finally concealing ourselves in shrubbery near the front wall. After a few passes back and forth on the lawn, they stopped not more than ten feet from us, and one with a pockmarked face turned and stared at me, virtually eyeball to eyeball.

But he didn't see me! He hadn't rotated his flashlight, and no moon meant he might as well have been staring into a black hole. The danger was being heard, not seen, and we remained as quiet as the startled crickets.

After what seemed an eternity—but could only have been a couple of minutes—the soldiers moved over to the walkway, and followed its length to the steps leading to the second floor where Vivian and the children slept. Would they be so bold as to barge into an American-owned inn at the SS-like hour of 2:15 in the morning?

They might. Then again, maybe not. Even powerful Thu Lee might wax reluctant over offending a strong Thai ally like the United States.

The soldiers paused. They exchanged a few words and I imagined they debated whether to go up the stairs.

They chose discretion. Instead of going up to the second-floor rooms, they walked the lower front portion of the building, then went to the rear side of the property. Finally—how to describe my relief?—they exited the compound via the gate. Perhaps thirty seconds later we heard the armored van crank up and saw its lights on the street as it faded into the Bangkok night.

We came out of the shrubbery, tense, wound tight, wondering if the danger was over, or if it had just begun.

"What do you think?" Scott asked.

"Nothing positive. I guess we can be grateful that we only lost a couple gallons of sweat."

"It sure wasn't good. Not when that ugly one was looking right at you."

"A high-stakes game, as they say, with several lives in the balance—Vivian's, the children's, and ours."

"Should we move them to another place?"

"No. We'd need Alice's van, and by the time she could get here it wouldn't matter. If the soldiers are coming back, they'd arrive before she could. Also, a sudden move would scare Vivian and the kids."

"You're right. She has held up good until now, but if she loses it you'll never get her through Immigration in the morning."

"Let's sit tight. Stay with our shift schedule."

That's what we did. The soldiers didn't return and morning dawned a welcome sight. The sun rose peacefully with the sounds of early traffic, and we prepared for the critical day ahead by optimistically packing our suitcases.

▲
Bangkok Guest House.

Vivian and the children ▶
at the airport.

18

A Small-Town Welcome

MONDAY, FEBRUARY 1, 1988. Ed Wehrli drove Vivian and me to Immigration, and we arrived right at 9 A.M. They went inside while I remained in the embassy car, searching each face that entered the office building, looking for Richard, or any COG members, who might be after us.

By 9:30 I was anticipating seeing them walk out, Vivian smiling ear-to-ear. It didn't happen, and I told myself I should be realistic: Even prodded by Wehrli's clout, government bureaucrats would not set speed records. Nevertheless, I grew increasingly anxious about Scott and the children. What if soldiers came back to the Guest House?

At 10:30, still no sign of Vivian or Wehrli. We should have been back at the Guest House by now to pick up the children and leave for the airport.

I couldn't stand it any longer. I entered the building and found Vivian and Wehrli cooling their heels inside the office that handles American passports.

"What's the holdup?" I asked.

"We've been waiting for them to reach Commander Kullama on the border," said Wehrli, "but it seems he's out in a remote area and can't be contacted by phone. We're hoping now that the next-in-charge can get this settled."

Waiting. Hoping.

"Maybe I can do some good upstairs," I said. "We're running out of time."

"I know. But I think this will be cleared up in a few minutes."

Upstairs I located Ayuthaya, who bowed as he greeted me. I thanked him for his help (no sense dwelling on his having given Richard those passports), and told him about our stalemate with the exit visa stamps. He made phone calls, then went downstairs where Wehrli still struggled to make the bureaucracy listen.

Ayuthaya talked with the officer handling the children's passports. He then took Wehrli and me to another office and pleaded our case in his native tongue. Wehrli talked to the new bureaucrat in Thai, and then we rejoined Vivian, while Ayuthaya stayed behind.

A few quiet minutes passed before Ayuthaya came out and said, "The passports will be cleared."

"We've done it!" I exclaimed foolishly. But it really appeared we had.

A man at a desk began processing the paperwork and I looked at my watch. We could still make the flight with a little time to spare, unless we hit heavy traffic.

About an hour later, at 11:45, the paperwork completed, we rushed to the office where it would be stamped by a captain.

Ayuthaya went in alone and came back shaking his head. He said, "The captain is at lunch and will not return until 12:30."

The normally cool and diffident Wehrli became assertive, demanding to talk with someone higher in rank. We were told to wait until the captain returned.

Out of deference to Wehrli, I decided against a phone call to Brad Backstrom, despite not being sure we could survive another day in Bangkok. Actually, I didn't hold out a lot of hope that Brad could help, at any time, much less at 1 A.M. in the United States.

The captain returned promptly at 12:30. Ayuthaya went in to explain that the passports were ready for the exit stamps.

Five minutes later Ayuthaya told us, "The captain is calling another captain; he will see us in a moment."

Ayuthaya pulled me to the side and said, "My friend, I must tell you the captain is afraid to approve the passports. Richard Shillander has come in and complained. The captain does not want to make a decision without approval from Commander

Kullama and wants to wait until he comes back from the border on Friday."

What could I do with Vivian and the children until Friday? Even then, we had no assurances. Ayuthaya's face mirrored the disappointment in mine.

At 12:45 the captain called us into his office. In broken English he explained that he did not have the authority to issue exit stamps "because of the confusion." He said we would have to wait until his commander returned, or until they could reach him for a decision.

Wehrli got hot. He insisted that they should let the children leave the country.

The captain said he had spoken with the other captain about the papers, and they agreed neither of them could be responsible for making the decision.

Wehrli, now steaming mad, asked if there was another superior officer he could talk to. The captain interrupted him to answer a ringing phone.

Wehrli looked at me and said, "I've never seen anything like this before."

The captain had come to attention and answered questions from the caller in a military manner. Wehrli smiled at me and said, "You did it." I wondered what I'd done.

Ayuthaya's face was wreathed in smiles. He and Wehrli told me the ongoing call was with the Minister of Foreign Affairs, one of the highest ranking officials in the country, and obviously he had received a communication from the Thai ambassador to the United States, who had phoned in the middle of the night at Senator Pressler's request.

The captain hung up and, without a word, stamped and signed the passports, then handed them to us.

I stood up with a step so light I felt able to leap across the ocean to home.

After all the pleading, cajoling, and arguing, it had taken one phone call and two minutes to clear up the entire mess.

We rushed out of the office, shouting thanks over our shoulders to Ayuthaya, and into the waiting embassy car. Seconds were precious: If we hit any serious traffic glitches, we would miss the plane.

On the way back to the Guest House, I apologized, not very sincerely, to Wehrli for any problems caused by Brad Beckstrom's intervention.

"Think nothing of it," he said. "You know, I never enjoyed a moment more than when I saw the expression change on that captain's face."

We reached the Guest House at 1:45. Scott had been pacing outside awaiting our arrival, and I gave him a thumbs-up. He quickly went to our room and brought down the luggage.

Alice and the crew also were there with cameras turning. When they heard the good news, they cheered.

After a scramble to load people and luggage into the vehicle, the ride to the airport was quiet. We watched the road, hoping it would stay clear, and pushed the speed limit.

We got to the airport at 3. Alice and her technicians had finished, and good-byes were tearful and necessarily short. I didn't have long enough to thank them for their help, but I think they knew how grateful I was. Alice and her "20/20" crew had been a bigger asset to the case than I had ever imagined. They had more than covered the story; they suffered with every negative turn, rejoiced with each shred of good tidings.

Scott, Vivian, and the children followed me through the airport lobby to the Thai Air counter. After the receptionist computed new passage for Scott and me, I turned to Vivian and asked for her tickets.

"I don't have one," she said in a pitiful voice.

"And the kids?" I asked.

"No," she replied meekly. When desperation drove her to come in advance to Thailand, she had been able to afford only a one-way fare for herself.

The reservationist tallied the airfare for five passengers at $5,226.48, and I felt a flicker of irritation. It passed quickly. Vivian simply hadn't had the money for a round-trip ticket for herself and four more to take her children home. She had done what any mother would: come as far as she could on what she had, and trust to faith. I paid for the five tickets.

We were trying to clear customs at 4:15 when the passports for April and Caleb were questioned by Immigration officers. It was a problem Wehrli had warned us about, those old snapshots. Ten minutes elapsed. Twenty. A ranking officer was summoned to eyeball the passports, and I nervously shuffled my feet, knowing if this continued we would be looking for a place to spend another night in Bangkok.

The customs officer in charge went from one child to another, taking his time comparing faces to pictures. Fifteen more minutes passed, and I thought I'd go mad. At last, blessedly, he stamped the papers and let us through.

We ran down the concourse in a wild stampede, scattering, as some raced faster than others. Scott sprinted ahead to stop the flight attendant from closing the door.

The stewardess smiled, and told him that another five seconds and he would have been too late. She held the door open, as one by one Vivian, April, John, Tito, and Caleb arrived at the boarding gate. Breathing heavily, they got on the plane, not fully comprehending that they were leaving Thailand behind to start life anew in a very different world.

Scott and I settled into our seats. He grinned and said to me, "You know it's not over until we're in the air, Mike."

I didn't need to hear that. As the plane taxied down the runway closer to takeoff, we sat still, wondering if the air traffic controller would possibly radio the pilot to turn around and return to the terminal.

At 5:30 P.M. Thai time, Flight 606 took off with a mother, her four children, and two contented, exhausted investigators onboard.

We survived, I thought. Scott and I tipped our drinks at the reunited family.

Air travel fascinated the children and kept their minds off the metamorphosis their lives were undergoing. April and the boys found many new worlds to explore aboard the jumbo jetliner. They marveled at the simplest gadgets—the fold-up dinner tray on the back of the seats, for example, which frequent flyers take for granted. And they considered the headphones piping pleasant music into their ears and an adventurous inflight movie to be state-of-the-art advancements in space-age technology.

Scott and I enjoyed the refreshing displays of naiveté from the Shillander children, but knew they would have a lot of catching up to do before being accepted by their more socially sophisticated American peers. Occasionally the beauty of their

ignorance was marred by reemergence of the intense program-
ming they had received from the cult and particularly from
Richard.

Landing and taking off in Hong Kong, San Francisco, and
Minneapolis entertained them with the curious miracles of
modern aviation.

In Hong Kong, when we browsed through the magnificent
duty-free shops, all wanted candy—Caleb's short-lived protest
forgotten. And in San Francisco the young Shillanders ended up
sporting Giants baseball caps.

Watching the children, getting to know them, if only for a
few days, I saw positive signs: smiles they wiped off their faces
when they thought I was looking, giggles when they examined a
new toy, one or the other of them snuggling with their mother
as we flew high above the Pacific Ocean. It all made me believe
that these young people whose lives we had touched would
grow up proud and strong, and pass along to others some of the
love and concern they received in their new life with Vivian.

On February 2, 1988, at 2 P.M., Scott and I saw our investigation end when we delivered Vivian and her family back to an
airport crowd of more than a hundred anxiously waiting First
Baptist Church parishioners and friends, including the youngest
Shillander, Yancha. He had never known his brothers and sister.

Television cameras recorded the happy scene, and a tearful, ecstatic Vivian talked to reporters. I felt better than ever
about the future of the children, watching their strong, decent
mother field with dignity questions from the press.

I knew the memories of our short stay in Sioux Falls would
forever remain fresh. They greeted us as only small-town folks
can, with hundreds of balloons, and plenty of loving support for
Vivian and the four little Shillanders. These people, too, had
shared the struggle and adventure of bringing the children
home.

Unfortunately, Scott and I couldn't stay for the church
party planned that night. We were due on that assignment in
Europe the next day. It was just as well. We had done what we
could. Now it was time to move on.

▲
Caleb, Tito, & April
on plane to Hong Kong.

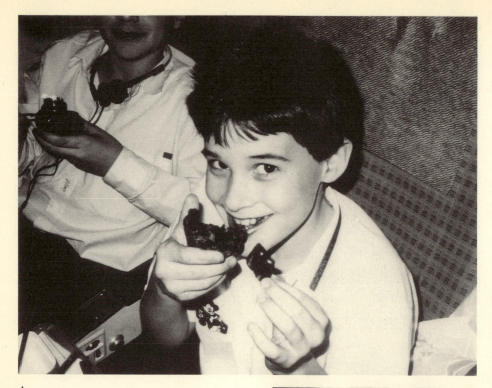

▲
Tito on plane to
Hong Kong.

April and crew waiting ▶
on parking lot.

▲
Vivian & April on the
plane to Hong Kong.

▲
Happy arrival in the
United States.

Epilogue

JANUARY 1990. I called Brad Beckstrom for a last update on Vivian and the children before putting this book to bed. Almost two years had elapsed since we'd brought them out of that Thai jungle.

Eager for progress reports, I had talked to Vivian periodically since we'd recovered the children, but on this occasion I wanted to hear what Brad had to say. He possessed the rare advantages of closeness to the family and deep concern for its welfare coupled with keen objectivity. During the first critical months in Sioux Falls, he had been a close counselor and valuable friend to the Shillanders, someone always available to listen, to *help*, during those tough early times of adjustment. Happily, though he continued to maintain a caring, big brother's eye on the family, the need for his role had decreased.

Brad was particularly happy this day to report that Vivian was about to enroll in computer training courses. We both thought it another important step in her odyssey out of the cold. The Children of God had consumed critical years of her life, time most people her age—*my* age—used to establish the foundation upon which their most lasting accomplishments were built. Ever since she dared that first brave stand against the COG in Asia, she showed she was made of special stuff.

And who could be disappointed by her staying power? Against terrific obstacles, she had kept her five children together, a woman alone (the church had helped, and concerned friends like Beckstrom, and she had found some government assistance—inadequate, of course—even the most flinty

179

hearted wouldn't have opposed or found ill-invested, but at bottom it was Vivian's victory).

"What about the children?" I asked Brad. The children. They were why we did all of this.

All of them are in school, Brad reported. They have made friends. They participate in and enjoy those activities—sports, scouting, television, trips to gut-buster fast-food emporiums—that comprise the bread and butter of their peers.

They are good kids, Beckstrom tells me, and not because I want to hear it. April particularly, he says, has developed a close, warm, very special relationship with her mother.

All of them are in school. I savored the line. They had refused to attend school when they first got to Sioux Falls. Who could argue that the children hadn't come a long way?

I asked Beckstrom, "What's the biggest problem they face now?" He answered, "They haven't yet completely adjusted to all the freedom an American family offers. They were accustomed to a very disciplined life filled with strictures. The Children of God directed their every movement."

I asked the most important question, and held my breath awaiting his answer. "Would they go back to COG if they had a choice?" Beckstrom repeated. "Oh, goodness, no. They much prefer where they are."

Which leaves just a few odds and ends for the reader.

Scott Biondo still works for Allied Intelligence, a good friend and valued employee; someone, as a U.S. president once said, you can go to the well with.

Most Children of God members won't talk to the press, and are even more loath to confide in me. I tried, though, and learned that the cult contends it has suspended the practice of Flirty Fishing, in part because of the AIDS epidemic. This is a claim I don't entirely believe.

And that leaves me. As I sat down to work on this epilogue, I was debating whether to go after COG again. A desperate grandmother had contacted my office—her grandson, a young boy, was trapped in the cult overseas. Would I bring him home?